A Force in Shoes

A journey to your higher self

Kevin Ireland

Edited by Nicola Kearns

Best wishes
Kevin Ireland

Copyright Information

All rights reserved. No part of this publication may be reproduced in any form or by any means - graphic, electronic or mechanical, including photocopying, recording, taping or information storage and retrieval systems - without the prior written permission of the author.

Photographs are author's own.

Author profile photograph on page 174 by Nicola Nea.

Edited and designed by Nicola Kearns

(www.leitrimwritingcottage.com).

Copyright © 2023 Kevin Ireland

ISBN 9798389462281

Table of Contents

	Page
Acknowledgments	7
Chapter 1. Slowing Down in Life	9
Chapter 2. Question Your Life	12
Chapter 3. Living a Simple Life	17
Chapter 4. Love	24
Chapter 5. Energy	34
Chapter 6. Fear	51
Chapter 7. Fear of Source	55
Chapter 8. Codependency	59
Chapter 9. Compassion	70
Chapter 10. Forgiveness	73
Chapter 11. Trust	77
Chapter 12. Mind	80
Chapter 13. Protecting Yourself	85
Chapter 14. Free Will	90
Chapter 15. Elements	96
Chapter 16. Freedom	110
Chapter 17. Loneliness and Lockdown	115
Chapter 18. Awake	119

Chapter 19. Healing	124
Chapter 20. Sound Healing	137
Chapter 21. Space	142
Chapter 22. Nervous System	147
Chapter 23. Know Thyself	152
Chapter 24. Our Limited Minds	155
Chapter 25. Reflections	161
Author Biography	176

This book is dedicated to my son, Nicholas.

Acknowledgements

There are some people I wish to thank who have played an important part in my life's journey. First of all I acknowledge the Source of all creation and intelligence for giving me life and working through me to create this book.

Thank you to my parents Mary and James, for all they have done and continue to do for me in my life. To my very well balanced in life brothers, John and James. To all the family and friends who are part of my life.

To my spiritual teachers/healers/mentors and friends; Pat Kelly - Dublin, Alison Byrne, info@alisonbyrnehealing.com - Dublin, Della Donnelly - Athlone, Mairead Murray - Cavan, Paddy Ward - Longford, Amanda Jenkins Doyle - Roscommon, Virginia Harton - Serenity Lodge, Cavan, Francis Molloy – www.innerwisdomhealing.ie Sharon O'Raghallaigh – The Healer Within – Mayo, Eileen Ireland for the secretarial work.

A special thank you to my editor, Nicola Kearns from www.leitrimwritingcottage.com without whose help this book would not have been possible.

CHAPTER 1

Slowing Down in Life

People really need to slow down to live genuine, peaceful and happy lives.

Life is for living, not chasing money or bills. Keep life as simple as possible. Be conscious when you are buying a car, a house or whatever. Ask yourself if it will really bring happiness? There is a lot to be said for renting a house instead of buying. If renting you can live and work anywhere in the world. You are not tied to a big mortgage repayment and all of the bills, house insurance etc.

Many employers have a lot of power over employees and power can create fear. Some managers often go for these jobs to make themselves feel important. Sometimes these people are on negative ego-based power trips. This is very common in the workplace. The bottom line is the employer being concerned only with power and money, with no respect for staff or their families. This does not happen in all businesses, but it is in some. Greed and competition will never produce a fulfilled life. I think if there were more people not saddled with big unnecessary bills, they would have a better quality of life, instead people are wishing their lives away – 'When I have this new car, or a big house etc', they think they will then be happy. Pleasure comes and goes. It is not lasting.

CHAPTER 2
Question your Life

Life awareness did not just happen for me either. I have experienced immense joy and happiness, to immense darkness, to a connection of bliss of unlimited peace, to small setbacks. I call these lessons in life.

Learn to trust yourself and not just other people. The best way in life is to spread love and to be love. We can all have an amazing life with practice and patience. Everyone has to carry their own weight. Life is to be lived like dancing; enjoying the dance and not thinking of the destination or looking for approval of your dance!

Be mindful what you watch on television. If it is not good, simply turn it off. You are always programming your subconscious mind, which is 90% of how you feel.

Who are you? Who is the higher power or the universe? What is the spiritual part of life? What is the human experience of past lives, patterns in families?

Everyone has to learn life for themselves. What is energy? What is consciousness? When did conditioning and illusions of life start? What is soul growth?

Seeing time as simply an illusion will make it easier to live in the now! Sometimes we keep thinking we should be doing more in life, be more aware that maybe we are doing enough. People should be living from the inside out, not the outside world in, and not attached to worldly things.

Ask yourself, 'Who am I?'

It is very easy to enjoy life, if you know who you are.

I do believe to a certain extent, we might have to get lost to find ourselves. It is part of the human experience of life - to have a true understanding of who we are, our purpose in life, our soul and growth, balance, spirituality, mentally, emotionally and physically.

There is a reason for everything.

Be aware that in this modern world, life is sometimes like a game of snooker, having to think four shots ahead. This alone can easily condition us to not live in the present, which is life. How would you reply if I asked you these questions?

- ♥ What is fear and sadness to you?
- ♥ If I asked you who you are?
- ♥ If I asked if you are spiritual?
- ♥ If I asked you what is love?
- ♥ If I asked you what is joy?
- ♥ If I asked you what is peace?
- ♥ If I asked you what is happiness?
- ♥ If I asked you what is pleasure?
- ♥ If I asked you what is life and who is your greatest Source?
- ♥ If I asked is it important to examine life from day to day deeply?
- ♥ If I asked is it important to treat earth with respect? Earth is part of us and we are part of earth. The universe provides life spiritually and physically.
- ♥ If I asked you why is your life out of balance?
- ♥ Why are so many people unhappy?
- ♥ Why are so many people on medication?
- ♥ Why are so many people alive but not living?
- ♥ Why are so many people codependent?
- ♥ Why is there so much education but little intelligence?

- ♥ Why so many people don't think properly?
- ♥ Why so many people have to be emotionally intelligent?
- ♥ Why so many are living from base levels?
- ♥ Why so many want to be controlling or control life?
- ♥ Why so many some people in powerful positions in religion, politics, college, media, wars, food, oil, chemicals, intense farming, haulage, companies, businesses and companies treat each other like property and not fellow human beings? This all leads to no life and loss of life.

Derrycarne Woods, Dromod, County Leitrim

CHAPTER 3
Living a Simple Life

The inner child is in everyone and is determined by the conditioning from past generations and your parents, family and schoolwork. Unconscious people will keep suffering unnecessarily until they start to examine their lives and take responsibility for themselves.

Why is primary school, called primary school? Most people do not know how to teach kids right from wrong, love from hate and greed from generosity. A lot of parents are too far gone themselves with the damage they have caused by a materialistic life. Children cannot be bought happiness, or have their own mind, their own life purpose, when mum and dad don't know themselves. Instead of parents teaching children about life, the children are sometimes dictating the parent's lives.

All this money has turned people on themselves. Money is important. It is part of life. It has its place, but it is not life. We are not a car, a house, or a holiday.

Do not be anyone else's property. Do not be your job, car or money etc. Everything in life is a spoke in a wheel and not the whole wheel.

Pleasures are important for nourishing souls. The thing is to not get attached to pleasures. They come and go. They come from outside of you. Inner peace, love, happiness comes from within.

Some people mix up pleasure with happiness.

Pleasures can turn into attachments, such as smoking for example. The person is getting a few moments of pleasure escaping pain; or they are low in energy because of a busy lifestyle and not choosing the correct choices in life.

This can cause negative emotions, maybe from a family pattern or a past life issue. That one cigarette a day becomes ten or twenty a day.

The subconscious mind is all the conditioning from past lives. From the day we are born it is energy in our body organs which records all our feelings. Most of our thoughts and actions and situations arise from the subconscious. The more that is not good in your life, the more negative energy builds up without proper guidance and awareness, acceptance and forgiveness is needed. The persons' energy will spiral more negativity. I think the further a person has gone from themselves sometimes through no fault of their own, depends on circumstances of family. For example, some wealthy families often do not know the importance of genuine family time. There is no importance put on family time and they are neglected or spoiled without balance.

The poor and the wealthy should all be the same, not classed. Humans should treat each other the same. Sometimes the wealthy man can be shallow and control people with fear. They identify themselves only with their business or status.

Poorer people are not exposed to what life is like for the rich with the status of job titles. A lot of people are easily led by companies and end up being controlled by bills.

A lot of genuine, big-hearted people are used and abused in their job, as they do not understand how one human being could be so cruel to another human being. Many unconscious people in the world try and bring people down to their negative energy. This comes from a place of fear, control and self doubt. If you have that feeling, you are in the wrong job. Leave the job as soon as you have another job to go to. It could also be a relationship or a family member. Be conscious of this.

Self-love is the most important. Rest, thoughts, correct food, and exercise - all in the right balance of course. Do not be running the roads or be in the gym day and night, escaping issues. If something causes you pain or fear it just needs to be checked. Ask where does it come from? It will keep coming up until it is embraced and healed. I recommend going to a good spiritual teacher/healer because they have walked the walk and know what they are about.

A spiritual teacher/healer is also a life coach, a good counselor, or a book like this is also a life teaching book.

This book walks you through darkness into light. Darkness should be embraced because it teaches you who you really are and pushes you into the right life. Then you actively realize the reason for the darkness. Take rest in winter and then bloom in the summer. You do not sleep with the light on. Whilst asleep, the intelligence in your body and mind are resting and nourishing you for another day. If you cannot sleep at night, do not fight this. It could be your energy changing.

See the intelligence of your body to operate itself. That is the creator of the universe or whatever you believe in. There is intelligence in the universe and in the earth. Earth is a living organ, giving life. There is nothing more intelligent as our higher self and our higher power that creates and operates this life. So it is important we do not get in our own way and think that we know everything.

Some say a chemical reaction created life. Look at the intelligence of our voice and all we created for good. This is not a chemical reaction. Intelligence is given to us by our Higher Source. It is up to us to use it correctly.

It is very important to know that suffering is your soul purging who you are not and to embrace the processes, instead of fighting it. Watch closely for the lessons, and then keep reminding yourself of the progress of love, peace and joy.

Do not think that you are going to be able to change everyone and the world when you make progress. Everyone has to take part in so many ways. This is all to change the pattern in society and prevent people from going in the wrong direction and to correct direction in life now, and for generations to come.

Finding Your True Self

CHAPTER 4

Love

There are so many types of love. Sometimes it is easier to love people and things, but it is very important to love ourselves from within and not be codependent on others or identify ourselves with material things in life. The more a person truly practices loving themselves, it is then that they will evolve to heaven on earth. When you find your true self, everything will fall into place. You will have an off moment every few days; that is simply life encouraging us all to grow even more.

I think most people suffer minor or major trauma in life at some stage. There is a reason for everything. That is your higher self making you dig deep into yourself. Anything negative is fear based. People take drugs for several reasons. It could be too much freedom in life, and they do not know how to balance that energy and emotion. This can lead to self destruction. I think for these people, they have to be taught the reason this happened.

Could it be that their higher self used the drugs to drive them to despair and stop patterns in their family life? Do they need this to find their true purpose and gifts?

Singers and artists can be very sensitive because they are heart-based people with a lot of emotions. This is where artistic people with talents and gifts arise from.

Everything is in the heart, so if you are having a tough day or a fantastic day, realize it is coming from your heart and the Source's intelligence is behind producing that emotion. For example, if you are in a wrong job, you will suffer until you are doing the job that is your sole purpose.

There are cases where people are mentally not able to work because of traumatic upbringings, where they were smothered with being controlled.

The inner child is in everyone and each child has to be given balance, not sitting on mom and dad's knee all day. A child, from when they are young, has to be allowed to express themselves, not in a spoiled way, as in looking for attention is not the same.

We are part of the process; making babies and nourishing them, teaching them manners, and right from wrong and taking responsibility. A child cannot be bought basics. Children should not be constantly looking into computer games. It is bad parenting to have allowed this to go on. This is programming a child for a life of fear and codependency. Children are sometimes distracted from themselves by parents to keep them quiet. In the end they cannot sit with themselves in peace. They are so long distracted from themselves. This leads to growing emotions of fear and a problem can develop in later life where they cannot live normal lives. This can ruin both their life and their communities.

A person who wants to change their life has to embrace where trauma came from, which most of the time was in childhood.

A good spiritual teacher/healer will put them on the right path of life. A person who suffered trauma will use their negative emotions, which is 90% of who we are, to push life away from themselves and push away the correct people from their lives. A true spiritual teacher/healer will connect them with themselves and they will then want to connect with the correct people in their life. It is all about waking up. Do not be a sheep and follow the flock. Be yourself. It takes time, pain and growth. But know that heaven can be experienced on earth. Everything happens for a reason.

The earth rests at night-time to nourish itself for growth the next day. It is the same for people. Everyone goes through periods of darkness. The reason this happens is for the person's soul to grow. It is not all negative like people think. If people were aware of this, then life will be so much easier for some of them. Darkness is another spoke in the wheel for people and everyone's life for growth. Be aware of this and focus on the lessons. Sometimes people put labels on themselves and get attached to these labels. Your Higher Source is forcing you to look deep within yourself, to find who you are and your purpose in life, so you can have a healthy relationship with yourself, your Higher Source, the people of the world, the earth and the universe. Know that you are connected to the universe. You are part of it. So, as the universe changes it affects you too. It is important to know this.

When you are troubled or looking for advice, try not to get in your own way. Know that the intelligence that operates your body and the Source is in you and all around you. Trust is very important. Trust in the Source and you will trust in yourself.

If you do not know the Source, he/she will create circumstances good, or not so good, so you properly learn about the Source within. If everything was straightforward we would be ignorant. This is why some people think they know everything, because they are ignorant. Stay away from these people and situations as best as you can. If you are friends with these people, you do not have to answer to them. Just leave quietly. Life will be a lot easier for you.

A spiritual teacher/healer changes a person's energy and how they feel about themselves. It is perfectly normal sometimes for a person to have a spiritual crisis because their ego is shattered, and the person is starting to see through the illusions and conditioning. A person could have been comfortable with suffering, because they were afraid of letting go of the experience. A life of bliss comes when you let go, forgive, and embrace the negative - waking up to whom you really are; which is a life force, energy, having a relationship with the Source, being part of the universe, and knowing your purpose, feelings of love and peace etc, is pure consciousness. You should have no crazy desire in thinking you will find who you are in a car, job or money.

You will be happy and content just being in the now, experiencing every moment with passion and even accepting the off days with understanding.

Keep falling and being in love with yourself and know that the Source is in you and all around you. Appreciate that you have the gift of life. Life is short on this planet. Put the Source where your heart is. The mind is only for doing things. The reason people's minds are so overactive, is because people are not educated. Money is only a spoke in the wheel. It is not the whole wheel. Some people are looking at all these restaurants, cars, types of food, all readily available on the phone, and it is all too much in people's faces. Their minds are fleeting from one thing to another for so long, that they are conditioned to work from the mind and not the heart. People are gone so far from themselves that they are lost and do not know what is going on; then they start looking for attention in all the wrong ways. They get in trouble with greed, people, loving things and not themselves, letting people use them. Companies, relationships, government, banks, police; every organization treats people like they are property, then the man or woman are not happy and blame each other, or try to control each other as though they own each other.

It is all fear-based, instead of love-based. This is what happens when people are conditioned to not know themselves. Some people in powerful positions are not helping because they are ego-based and on pathetic power trips. Sadly this pathetic ego is fear-based. It is fake-based and has become acceptable all over the world, in every walk of life. It takes a lot of suffering to wake people up, and when some people in powerful positions can keep getting away with this, I would say they are the most ignorant people in the world with no conscience. Some are blind to their fake-ego that gets hungrier the bigger the ego gets. Unconscious people are never happy. They do not know themselves.

Everyone has to learn to love themselves as life goes along and everyday that love has to be self nourished. It is hard for parents to encourage a balance of love in this modern world. Love cannot be bought. Parents sometimes are too busy to know themselves; they try to make up for this by buying kids everything to create happiness, instead most of the time this creates codependency. Love is an emotion and has to be expressed that way to children, and sometimes children and adults have to earn that love by being taught manners and respect. Keep life simple and make time quality time for yourself and your children. Love is everything. Do not take this gift for granted. Genuine love is not codependency

Do not look for your own happiness in your children. Show them how it is done by example, because if you are not living as a conscious parent, it will show in the children and in their adult life; they will then unconsciously make you feel guilty for your lacking as a parent. This cycle will repeat itself again and again until genuine love is restored.

Codependency could be from being dependent on another person, being a workaholic, addiction to alcohol and or drugs, religion and money - anything that is not in balance.

Sadness is the Source telling you to examine your life. All these problems are not as negative as you think. They are lessons to wake you up to life. It is an awareness to know this. Life is in our breath. That is how close you are to bliss at all times.

Every child has to learn the basics in life, to cope in this vast materialistic modern world. When children are not taught the basics they sometimes get lost, or are lost souls in adult life. The inner child is in every adult.

If anyone thinks they are better than another person or looks down on another person, they have a lot to learn. When we are adults, sometimes we get feelings we are not comfortable with. This can be conditioning from childhood (our inner child). Our adult self has to correct our inner child.

Rosses Point, Sligo

CHAPTER 5

Energy

Focus on your energy. What *is* good energy? Are your thoughts good? If not, what is the lesson here? Is it something from a past life? Do not be addicted to negative thinking. Be aware and watch all sources, that they are nourishing and embracing negative energy to turn it into positive energy. It is also important to 'dose yourself for parasites'. They can eat up all the nutrients and cause tiredness, anxious feelings, and lack of energy. Feeling is energy. That is how we are to be at peace and love based, in line with the creator within us and all around us. You can see the universe in a person's eyes.

Remember the feeling and energy of joy and anything good is possible.

If you are not feeling good, the first thing is go to the doctor to make sure you do not have an illness, infection or disease. If you get the all clear, then it is a spiritual issue, which is a blessing and lesson in disguise. If you are not in a correct job or do not know your purpose in life; you will have inner turmoil until you do find your purpose in life.

You have to learn to be your unique self. Nobody owns you. Rest. Proper breaks are very important and do not to be looking into the phone all the time. Looking too much into the phone causes stress and anxiety. It is conditioning the person to be in the past or the future; and not in the now. It causes the mind and emotions to work overtime. Detaching people from themselves causes poor quality of life and decision making. Get out into nature and chat with friends and colleagues. If you cannot talk to other people, close your eyes or relax in nature and just be. It slows down emotions and thoughts. Accept we are in the here and now and simply enjoy our here and now. There is no tomorrow promised for anyone, so cherish every moment. Accept everything just as it is and no matter what it is going on in your life, know that it is meant for you at that time, to learn and for your soul's growth.

We are 80% water, so it is important to spend time near water and trees. If your heart is all over the place, think with your heart that you are like a tree. Imagine yourself rooted in the ground, connected to mother earth firmly. You are just like the tree breathing in fresh air; let go of thoughts, emotions and let the creator heal and rest you, and fill you with clean air. Do this for fifteen minutes when needed, even when slightly needed. Don't wait until you are exhausted, or it will take a long time to relax and let go and enjoy the gift of life.

There is no point looking for everything outside of yourself, when everything you need is inside you, in your inner world.

Everyone is learning in life, so do not take anything anyone says or does personally. Live like a rebel, living and expressing who you really are. When you know who you are, you will not disrespect yourself or allow anyone else to. You are not an organization or somebody that a company thinks they can own.

Those who identify themselves only with their job or any kind of organization, can be dangerous. You do not have to be the sheep. If you were meant to be an organization or owned by a job, we would all be the same. That is why our Creator made us all to look different; because we are, and we all have our own life purpose!

If you are feeling tired and fed up a lot, do not say that you are depressed or anxious. These words are how people put labels on themselves. If you are really tired, then your energy is stagnant. Do not keep lying down or sitting crouched. This is not good for a flow of energy. Sit up straight, walk straight, exercise, no matter how much you do not want to exercise. After a few weeks sticking it out you will have lots of self-esteem and lots of love for life. Energy will flow freely. We are all energy.

Even if you do not want to get up every morning, thank your Creator for the gift of life. Thank your spirit guides and angels. Over time you will see the massive change in your life. You do not have to know everything. Trust in your Creator, the universe and the Source.

A good cry sometimes lets go of the build-up of negative emotions. But you know the reason for crying, so do not identify yourself with sadness.

A man and a woman's eggs are half and half of the ingredients of making a baby. So a mother and father's lifestyle and diet are important, not to contaminate the ingredient to make that baby.

Too much indoctrination of any subject causes attachment, which leads to suffering. Indoctrination, a lot of the time, gives a person a mind-based limited belief way of living and causes a lot of suffering. The more they suffer, the more they feed themselves with limited or false beliefs, because it is a false ego they have identified themselves with. This is another example of living from the outside in. It is only from the inside that a person knows themselves. Suffering can make a person look inside themselves.

Sometimes in life a person finds it easier to concentrate more on people around them, than to concentrate on themselves. I think it is important for the person who is feeding this unwanted concentration to be aware that this person is actually reflecting themselves, otherwise the victim could unconsciously take on unwanted responsibilities, feelings, energy, which are all fear-based. When a person is pushing their concentration on you, it is important to clarify if it is for the better or not? Take action if needs be. Boundaries need to be set, or what is the lesson in this? Are they bringing up awareness to something? Are they bringing up awareness to identify limited beliefs, to negative self-introspection, lack of self love, lack of balance in life, exercise, proper meals, sleep, lack of self-respect, responsibilities for self, lack of awareness and understanding for self? Meditation is important a few times a week for self-love as it soothes your nervous system and relaxes the mind.

A relaxed mind can see things clearly. Meditation is important also for your true nature and for nourishing your inner world source, your Creator. It is important for receiving messages for your highest good. You might get a knowing during meditation, or in time when you are ready to receive information. Sometimes we have to purge unwanted beliefs and healings first. The thing is to know there is a reason for everything and to remind yourself every day of the reason, and trust the process is for your higher good. Do not try to control the process. Go with it. Take spiritual healing sessions, frequencies, meditation, believe in self-love and forget self-pity.

A spiritual teacher/healer and spiritual books like this one will bring awareness. Sometimes a person's limited belief, sickness etc, is passed on through generations. Sometimes people get comfortable with suffering and become afraid to let go of suffering, because they know nothing different, without awareness.

Society alone can bring people down. If not nice people come into your life, they will enter for a reason; for you to help them and them to help you, even if the person causes you great suffering, they are in your life for a reason. An important lesson to know is to choose wisely the people you let into your life. Maybe the job you are in is not your purpose in life. This is obvious when you notice you have grown and have nothing in common with the people you work with anymore.

Maybe you see that they identify themselves with their job and they are not spiritually awake. Perhaps you are becoming spiritually awake and looking for more meaning in life. You will not have deep conversations with these people. Small talk frustrates you. Do not rush the change in your life path. It takes a lot of unlearning to undo all the conditioning and to learn the truth of who you really are at the same time. That is why it is important not to rush this process, or it will take longer and complicate life more.

Roughly 80% of people do not know how the mind works. 80% of those think they know everything and believe their way of thinking and behaving is 100% correct and that everybody else is the problem. Some people are conditioned to think that life and the world revolves around them. Many of these people are narcissists. Some may be known as 'the black sheep in the family' and have all sorts of problems because they are not taught right from wrong, love from hate, give and take, manners or respect for themselves and everyone else. They are not let stand in their own two feet, or shown how to express themselves with dignity and confidence etc. Their parents believed they could buy their children's upbringing instead of teaching children the basics in life and show examples of humility. When parents identify themselves with everything outside themselves, they are lost souls living from the outside in, instead of the inside out. How could a child of that world be okay?

There are so many people asleep at the wheel of life and ego-based. Look at some people in powerful positions all over the world who think they own people and are on petty power trips.

These people are meant to lead by example; instead they are full of greed. It is no wonder there is no humanity in most places in the world and it is down to their false-ego. Money is important in the correct hands, but so many people identify themselves by money and materialistic things and do not appreciate what life truly is.

There are a lot of people suffering in the world due to ignorance and a lack of responsibility from parents, who only get defensive when their adult children start having problems. They say it couldn't be their fault, but it is, because they are just part of the 80% who are asleep at the wheel of life. Look at the amount of people who get married and do not know why, only because everyone does. They just tick boxes in life.

This book is to educate people of the world to understand suffering and guidance in truly finding themselves.

The reason so many people suffer is due to conditioning. People need to look back to childhood for where they are in life. They need to take responsibility for themselves and be rid of the limited belief and all they fear. Depression and sadness is the start of the death of the false-ego. Ego is just what the mind has been taught. It is false and not your true mind. The key importance for the person suffering is to distance themselves from the mind and anything fear-based. Keep reminding yourself that it is ego, not me. It is ego that has the whole world in chaos. I think that some people in powerful positions want people to be ego-based, fear-based and ignorant so they can control people to feed their own ego. They do not want people to wake up to themselves. For example, I think this is why they allow people to sell and buy cheap alcohol.

There are more people waking up every day, because they cannot handle the suffering any longer. The soul is pushing people through a 'dark night of the soul' which is devastating, but it is better in the long run. People wake up to the conditioning and find their true selves with the help of spiritual teachers/healers, meditation mantras, nature; eating root-based food is important for people going through 'dark night soul awakening', because it is in tune with the truth of life.

Purging the old and embracing new life, becoming spiritually aware of themselves and life around them through the energy of places and other people, they realize their own energy and the energy of the universe.

These people are sensitive to positive and negative, but when these people grow spiritually they choose jobs, people and places carefully. It is very important for spiritual awareness and awakens people to enjoy life.

Like a wheel of a bicycle for example, one spoke for exercise, one for pleasure, one for enjoying nature, one for the positive self-talk, one for meditation, one for work ... For some people, life is all exercise or work. It has to be a balance, not to identify themselves with something outside themselves.

Sensitive and unconscious people have to investigate their lives and where habits come from; what are they trying to escape from? When we are stressed we turn to habits for example, coffee. I actually think coffee is a dangerous drug if a person drinks too much of it. It causes anxiety and mood swings which can manifest in so many ways. One coffee a day is enough. If some people in powerful positions do not know the damage coffee is doing to mental and body health, it is out of ignorance. People are so stressed from disastrous upbringings. People are used for small money and shift work and big businesses insatiable greed. People are used, hence forcing people to attachments. People are waking up to life, buying more organic food and cooking at home when they have the time.

Ego is the most important topic. It takes time for people to learn what is happening and for their energies to change and understand the energies that nourish them; understand boundaries, responsibility, self love, awareness and understandings. All of these are important; especially to be your own person, stand in your own shoes, soul retrieval and cutting ties energetically.

People need to be aware of the nature of stubbornness. For example, if you are not happy doing a job, do not stay in it. Find a job you love and you will find like-minded people. Avoid any jobs that are against the grain of life if possible. We were never meant to be working at night. Do not sell yourself short for Pete's sake in any way. Every time you give yourself away, you are giving away part of your soul and who you are. You will suffer and you need to stand back and cut ties with people and your soul will be retrieved.

When people are handed everything by parents or some people in powerful positions while growing up, they are conditioned to think the world owes them.

They become codependent and throw tantrums in work when they should be delighted to be able to do a day's work to support themselves and their family. This is the ego again.

There is boredom from tiredness. People have to keep awareness for their own personal health.

To have and keep balance in life, eat properly, get proper sleep, avoid night shift work if possible. Exercise is very important, leisure, socializing and reading are all relaxing and very important. We need rest time for the mind and meditative music. Nourishment for the soul is more important than anything in the world. Our life is to nourish our inner world and not ego or attachments.

People should have a natural awareness to be content when they have enough and be aware to the illusion that they will be happy with more. Ignorance and greed are the most dangerous things to humanity and earth. We are here to evolve and grow in ourselves and to evolve to unconditional self-love. When we have self-love and respect and are not codependent, our purpose here is then to love and nourish the planet earth. Planet earth is our home and produces food, water, air, life for us and all creation. Divinity is in the soil. There is intelligence in soil to produce vegetables, trees for air, etc. There is intelligence in a tree, roots going down into the earth, getting nourishment of soil and water. It then produces life above the ground to support us with fresh air. Look at the trees and the birds. Everywhere you look is an expression of intelligence of the Creator and the universe. Just like the same intelligence inside us all. We are no more important than animals; we are just given a gift of more intelligence for us as human beings to evolve and nourish ourselves and planet earth in a healthy way. Not to take the Creator or the universe for granted.

We should not think that we know everything; we must get to know who we really are as a person spiritually, mentally, emotionally and physically. This is why so many people are lost, as they are looking up to leaders all around the world that are just ego-based and not soul-based. These people are so ignorant. They think they can destroy lives and earth to satisfy an unquenchable thirst for status, greed and petty power trips. If these people actually know themselves, they would have no false-ego or greed and we would not have intense farming, for example.

They are destroying water which is our main source of life and filling it with chemicals; but when farmers, for example, don't know themselves, they look to some people in powerful positions and leaders who are ego-based. Some farmers are conditioned to become ego-based to have more intense farming than his neighbor; then his neighbours sometimes end up in competition with each other. On it goes. Political leaders are creating separation around the world so as to easily control some people and feed their own egos.

The best thing to do is to buy food from markets and small shops and get back community spirit; make time for each other for the better. If you are gossiping, you have more work to do on yourself. Never look down on anyone or think you are above anyone. The intelligence of the Source to create a universe is in me, you and everyone, in everything on planet earth and the universe.

Embrace dark times. They are happening for you and not *to* you. They are to enable you to wake up to who you are. You probably will have to go through a 'dark night of the soul' if you are not living from the inside out. Trust the process and embrace letting go of the conditioning and embrace the rebirth. When you have your spiritual awakening, then you will realize the amazing creation you are. You are an important part of all creation. When you are spiritually awake you have a purpose to spread genuine love to everyone and everything. When you meet people who are not as evolved as you, love them, but have your boundaries at the same time. Do not take on other peoples' responsibilities when they are not responsible for themselves, due to conditioning, being spoiled by parents or some people in powerful positions; not being shown enough love and taught how to think right from wrong, love from hate, greed from generosity - most people do not have the basics in life. This is important when young. When we leave college, people think they know everything, when sometimes college conditions some people to be ignorant. They know how to answer a question, but not enough about the subject or lecture to last in the real world. They are ticking boxes basically.

Reality, going from college to a working life is a major change in anyone's life. Do not identify yourself with what you studied in college. It is not your life. It is just a job to pay the bills.

You have to be aware of people's energy, places, type of work, type of society etc. You have to have major awareness to these energies over time as they can cause severe trauma or bliss. Choose everything, everywhere and everyone with great awareness. Even our type of footwear and clothes changes our energy. For example, shining our shoes gives us a pride in ourselves. Know how to tune into energy and how to handle it.

It is important to empty ourselves of thoughts and feelings, usually by sitting in silence doing nothing. This is when your soul speaks and when your creation speaks.

It is also important to empty yourself to just being alive, nothing else. No thoughts or feelings. Then you have no labels or judgment and are just living in the present. There is bliss in just being alive in the present because all else is an illusion of thoughts/feelings/judgment. Sunday is a great day for most people to practice emptying. Do not view feeling empty as feeling nothing as a person, but empty of clutter in life; so your soul can speak whether it is in expressing creativity, new ideas, or enlightenment. This is when you are most pure, without expectations, desires or limits.

CHAPTER 6

Fear

Most of the time fear is an illusion inside each of us; and most of the time it is not real on the outside, it is an inner emotion. When a person truly wakes up to this, they are free and can replace that fear with love and joy. Listen to music, sounds of a natural heartbeat, mellow, dreamy, relaxing music with good lyrics.

Music is good and important for lifting the positive energy of the soul and changing negative emotions to positive. It helps a person let go and be free. Music is a gift from our Creator to nourish our souls and bring positive emotions alive.

If fear is a problem, no matter what anyone says or does, it doesn't matter. If it affects your inner world, you have to realize it is you annoying yourself. You need to heal that emotion by letting go and be yourself. With time you will not care what people say or think. Some people do not know how to handle too much time on their own. That is from fear. That is all. They are in a negative cycle and need to break free from that cycle. We cannot control what people say or do. Let it go.

When you have an illusion of emotional fear about something practice, accepting the fear as a lesson, which it is. Accept the fear as a reason to make you look deep within you, to make you learn to love yourself. That is the whole reason, for you to love yourself and grow into your purpose in life. Learn to relax by being still.

Life is a journey. Keep moving on that journey; keep that fire burning in your soul with love and strength. Every person in the world is on their own journey in life. Believe that you are part of that journey with consciousness. Sometimes it can seem like an uphill struggle for a very long time. When you find your feet, it will all be so much sweeter and that will last. There will be true peace and happiness. It will not be just a fleeting happiness coming and going. That is pleasure.

That is why so many unhappy people are putting the cart before the horse, looking for happiness in pleasure. True happiness comes from peace and love from the soul and knowing thyself.

Remember all the chaos across the world comes from fear. There are so many people and countries in competition with each other. Enough is never enough. We are all the one source of life. If everyone on a daily basis avoided fear, even low energy conversations, people would not be conformists. They would begin to think for themselves for the better and then people of the world would not be feeling fear.

CHAPTER 7

Fear of the Source

The fear of the Source in human beings is the intelligence within us when we are not in line with our true selves; or when we are in danger or near it, you will have the feeling of fear within. The Source has given us these fears to learn and grow. Most people do not realize this and suppress fear with drink, drugs, money, greed and so many other things. The most dangerous of all is people. People push their own fear onto others which manifest the suffering, because people do not know the reason for the fear or what it is. Some religious and government organisations have caused untold emotional trauma and suffering. There are some people in these organisations that need to take account and take action, instead of simply giving lip service. They are destroying their own identity by not taking action. Religions are very good for teaching people who they are spiritually, when people are conscious, and not just turning up.

People should be mature enough to see how special every person in this world is. There are some people in powerful positions who are destroying themselves, but it is people outside the organization whom they are quick to blame. People and organisations are too far gone from themselves and all the suffering they have caused. Instead they continue to lie to themselves.

When you wake up to the people that were asleep in life along with you, they will try to pull you back to sleep with them. It is difficult letting people go in life, but realize that they are holding you back. When they finally let go of you and you of them, you will feel the benefit of letting go of negative energy. Find a spiritual group. These people have had many 'dark night of the soul' awakenings and they will help and encourage you to become you. They will not control your life. They work from their heart and from divinity.

Get out in nature and do lots of walking. Eat less bad food. Bad food drains the soul.

Smile and spread unconditional love. A church can be good for silence, but you do not have to be a part of it. That is your business. Sitting in the silence of a church away from the busyness of the world gives your soul time for rest and comfort.

Be comfortable with not knowing a lot about life and why this and that. It is important to not want to know everything, because we are not capable of knowing everything. If you think you do know everything, you try to control life instead of having it in order. When you control every aspect of life, you try to control areas of life you do not like and how you react to this causes anxiety and suffering.

Strokestown House, County Roscommon

CHAPTER 8

Codependency

Codependency in relationships and with alcohol or drugs comes from fear. The person who is not educated about life is a lost soul. They need to be taught how to find themselves when walking this path alone. We all have our own path and lessons. Life does not just fall into place. I know some people are brought up being treated as though they are always correct and know everything, for example; some organizational leaders who believe their own lies, because they were brought up to think they know everything, when they do not even know themselves. People of the world are waking up to all false organisations whom actually think they own people and think they have the right to control people's lives; yet they do not know who they are themselves. It is just an inflated ego.

A lot of people are waking up to whom they really are and the knowledge that everything they need is inside them. When they realize the spirit of the Source is in them, they gain intelligence in the mind, body and heart. Follow your heart. They lose fear and they get their true identity of divinity, true intelligence of love and purpose. They lose all codependency. It is important to have awareness and a full perception of divinity in us and all around us and in nature. Look outside and see the amazing sky, grass, trees, mountains, lake, sea, animals and feel the breeze of fresh air. Go outside no matter what the weather is and enjoy true life. This is all we need. Too much of materialistic, superficial things have people conditioned to be too mind-based not heart-based. Stay in tune with nature. If you are a mature person that was, or is lost, give yourself time. Everything takes time. Get in tune with nature. When out walking, instead of looking down, look up and change your thoughts to the awareness of creation. You are part of this creation. That tells you how special you are. This practice will help you let go of the ego-mind.

When you notice there is a gap between yourself and negative thought; that is when you realize you are not the negative thought. When thoughts come and go, take notice where they are coming from. They are from memory; they are not from where you are sitting in that present moment. There is a gap between them and you. They are not you. They are just thoughts, just memories, just conditioning that you identify yourself with. So then go back to where you conditioned yourself with false beliefs and see who you were before you latched onto the illusion of false belief. The thing is not to fight negative thoughts, just have awareness that negative thoughts are only thoughts. That is all.

Do not run from fears or anxiety. They are just a negative emotion. Feel the fear. Accept it is how you feel in that moment and that is perfectly okay. Just see it as a lesson to keep nourishing your inner world with positive thoughts, music, good food, rest, exercise and good friends, spiritual teachers/healers and counselors. Books and reading are good for the mind and retraining the mind and feelings to be in the present.

Listen to your heart for the truth of intuition. If you listen to your mind, there is a chance of lying to yourself. When you have balance in your subconscious and conscious mind, you will learn or notice your intuition guiding you by feeling it is separate from a conscious mind, but guided by consciousness. You have to keep practicing self-love, without being codependent on anyone or anything, while keeping social contact with people who are good for you. It is important to cut negative people out of your life. You do not owe anyone your time. Some people will try to keep you trapped by being controlling and putting you on guilt trips. Set yourself free and keep healthy boundaries for yourself. You have to take responsibility for yourself and do not expect everything to be perfect in life. Always through life, learn to embrace good and the not so good. See the not so good times as a blessing or a lesson. The purpose of all of this, no matter how much pain it is for you, is to evolve to your purpose in life as a better person and to help people of the world around you evolve; and help planet earth, our temporary home. It is not all about the *I*. It is about us; the life that is in you is in me and everyone and everything. It is to be awake to realize that you are a part of this miracle called life.

Whenever you are in times of difficulty, remember you are part of this miracle. Listen to your intuition and not the ego-mind. Keep bringing yourself back to that intelligence. It is always there; full of love and support; no matter what.

Be very careful what you feed your conscious mind through your thoughts. Your thoughts cannot be correct if you do not nourish yourself with good food. Root vegetables are very important. If you are not happy in a job, leave your job as soon as possible, once you have another job first. If you are being bullied in a job or used in any way, report to the correct authorities within the company or other relevant bodies.

Sometimes owners of companies are owned by what they control, so they lose touch with themselves and become fear-based and full of anger. Nice people do not understand this. They have morals and get manipulated. Some owners and managers actually think they own people just because they work for them and can treat people any way they want. Greed and power trips are fear-based energies; not love-based, so they spread fear. In most places of work like this there are lots of conformists and when you are not a conformist, it is easy for you become a target of bullying.

Justice is very important. More than you realize. These people try and sometimes do, take away your life by pushing you into not feeling good enough and introduce emotional trauma. This is some of the reasons we have people committing suicide, developing drink problems etc. These people have suffered emotional trauma in life.

If you are one of these people, it is important to report to a solicitor for advice because you have to get justice for yourself. You could continue the rest of your life feeling let down and incomplete, plus it will leave work a better place and make the bullies examine their own life. Forgiving these people is important, because these people do not know who they are or what life is about. It is another form of sickness. Sometimes and a lot of times, we attract people into our lives that are the opposite of who we are. Everything is for a reason. First of all, it is to teach us and remind us who we are and to give us inner strength and courage. By knowing ourselves we are reminded that we are not this type of person. If I react to this person, what needs healing in me when I react? You need strong, firm boundaries to remove these people from your life and to protect yourself from mental and emotional abuse.

That is self-power; removing people from your life. Without talking negatively, walk away and give the other person love and forgiveness. This is the art of letting go without judgment.

Because some people are asleep at the wheel of life does not mean they are bad people, it just means they have to wake up to who they are and why they are here. Sometimes, these people try to abuse or use other people, when they are actually crying out for help and understanding, but they do not realize this themselves.

You can offer to help them, but be very aware that these people will make you feel responsible for them. Do not give too much to anyone, especially the people closest to you. You will condition them to take you for granted. People will respect you when you have a firm voice and boundaries. You cannot control the life of others. Everyone has to stand in their own two shoes.

Suffering is very important, just as much as happiness; most of the time we will not learn the basics in life without suffering and most importantly understand the reasons for suffering. Suffering is a blessing and until you understand that you will not have a solid foundation in life. Embrace suffering like you love it, because you know it is teaching you for the better, to create miracles and for you to realize the miracle you and everyone else is. For instance, sit in silence and think of the miracles you have such as eyesight, hearing, taste, touch, love, smell, a mind of your own and a heart for truth. When a conscious person has done a lot of work on themselves, they receive the gift of intuition, which is most important. It is divine guidance from within.

A lot of people have been spoiled by money in the wrong hands. This created a lot of ego, so if anyone looks down on you or blanks you because they think they are above you, understand these people have a lot to learn and do not take this behavior personally. There are a lot of people who have not a clue about life; the same life that is in me, you and in everyone else. The person on the street could have more life in them than the businessman or woman. That could be the reason for the homeless person on the street; maybe they could not cope with the fakeness in the world. Anyone can wear a suit.

Love yourself and practice self-love from your heart, instead of having an ego and a 'poor me' attitude. That is not love. When you love yourself, spread love by wearing a lovely smile for strangers.

People might think you are mad, but smiling and giving love can be more contagious and fun. People are falling into a stereotype of fakeness. The new and cool thing to do is to spread genuine love, because remember that life that is in other people, is also in you. The love you are giving will return to you. You will have a genuine confidence, because you live life's' truth. Just keep your boundaries in check. There is always someone to best you and teach you for the better.

Getting to know your intuition is important. You will express love, no matter what people say or do. You will be authentic. You will have a fire and strength of life coming from within. You will embrace ups and downs and everything in life, like surfing a wave. You will enjoy the power of life. The unstoppable force within you will take you completely out of your comfort zone. When you have sleepless nights, you are growing enormous strength inside. You will be shocked and surprised that the nerves built up of adrenaline from within, will direct a fantastic performance. This could be applied to sport, a court hearing, an exam etc. All these sleepless nights are your soul wanting to grow and express your truth or teach you a lesson; whatever the reason, it always for the better. I have seen it so many times, the more nervous you are, the better the performance. Do not doubt yourself. Your spirit will perform unlimitedly compared to your human aspect of life.

Conscious breathing is very important. It is like learning how to drive a car - you consciously have to learn to change gears, work the pedals, control speed and the car engine revs. It is the same with a person. You consciously learn deep breathing instead of shallow breathing when you get nervous. By doing conscious breathing in difficult times over a period of time just like driving the car, you change gears without thinking, because you have it programmed into your subconscious mind to do so. So with breathing, your subconscious mind will do conscious breathing itself, catching anxiety with a breath before it goes to your head. With subconscious breathing, your anxiety will pass faster over time with no lasting efforts. You will be aware that you do not have that uncontrollable feeling any longer, as your breath and breathing recovers it for you. It is important that we are aware of the air we are breathing in life and be very grateful.

Tarmonbarry, County Roscommon

CHAPTER 9

Compassion

One of the things with compassion is that when a person suffers trauma and unhappiness you can fall into self-pity easily. Even when you have recovered from emotional, mental, physical and verbal abuse, the thing is not to be too sympathetic with yourself and importantly other people. They will see you as too soft and try and push their problems onto you, or take you for granted. Do not let other people take you for granted. It is very important for self-respect to have boundaries and justice when it comes to compassion. Your time here is as important as everyone else's in this life. Every minute you doubt yourself, remind yourself of the gift of life you have been given, which is something which most people take for granted. Be bold in yourself by not backing down and be strong. It is quite easy when you become spiritually awake, and remember when we get tired it is normal to be weary. Our mental health needs to be tended to daily and if it is not good, remember it takes nurturing every day.

When we have compassion we are living from the soul because it is a feeling of life deep within us all. It is a feeling of love given to us all to create and nourish life, not just *I* mentality. But in every human, every living thing on earth and planet earth itself is a living source. The elements; soil, water, air, fire, all grow the food we eat which turns in humans when we consume. Have compassion for earth. It is our life's source and all created by our Higher Intelligence, God, Creator or the Universe; whoever you believe your life source to be. Have compassion.

CHAPTER 10

Forgiveness

From a young age children should be taught forgiveness. Because of a lack of teaching in life at a young age, a lot of adults have to be reminded to forgive themselves every few minutes, hours, days, weeks, months and years; also to forgive the people that hurt us intentionally or unintentionally. In this modern world I am guessing 80% of people are ego-based and not soul-based, so it is important to know what genuine forgiveness is and not just self-pity. If a person thinks life is all about them, they wonder then why they turn in on themselves in a very wrong way and blame everyone else. It is up to yourself to create your own life. It takes a lot of work on yourself sometimes, but if you want to be forgiving you have to put in the work. There is no such thing as a perfect life and therefore no such thing as a perfect upbringing. If there was, you would never learn to stand on your own two feet and discover the purpose in life and find true self-peace and love. It is important to forgive, even when you are spoiled and think that you know everything.

That is when you will realize someday that you need to forgive yourself for not knowing what you know now.

When you are truly awake, you will sometimes trigger the people that are still asleep because of conditioning. Forgive these people. Even if you triggered these people, they are unconsciously getting a blessing from you to wake up and grow in their own lives. Do not take on their negative energy or react. Instead, understand them in your own mind and walk away without reacting. This is true self love and realization in the power of knowing who you are. Do not try to fix anyone. When people truly want help they will look for it, in the meantime they will blame everyone else. Be aware that some employers can be controlling. For example, if this is the case, find another job with more enlightened people. Forgive them. It is the correct thing to do for self-worth and humanity.

Keep life simple as possible and then you will have less politics in life. You do not have to look up to any government or organization like they own you. Every town, city and village is being turned in the wrong direction by some people in powerful positions, to keep people down so they can control them. When people in power are controlled by constant brainwashing on television, radio and social media they are controlled by fear and they do not even realize this. People turn on themselves and everyone else is wrong. There are a lot of people waking up and I think as time goes on, all the suffering will cause people to wake up.

When you wake up, it takes time for your energy and emotions to change and for your subconscious mind to know itself again. Your soul will then speak the truth to your intuition, The Source, the universe, or whatever intelligence you believe in. The same intelligence is for everyone in the world. We all have different names for the intelligence that gives us life.

I have looked everywhere outside myself for happiness. After so much suffering and looking, I found the intelligence *within me* to give me everything. Now that I see the expression of intelligence outside me, life is bliss. I see the unknown as amazing. Even if nothing happens I see it as amazing, because to experience and observe Divine Creation that is in *us* and all around us is amazing to be a part of.

Kilglass, County Roscommon

CHAPTER 11

Trust

Do not live your life wondering who you can trust, because most people do not know themselves and you will have no trust in yourself. You have to get to know yourself, live from the inside out, do work on yourself and gain a lot of life experience. Trust is when you know how to listen to your own intuition. Intuition comes from the Source, the creator, the universe; it is the true intelligence of the soul. It is the intuition we live from, not the ego-mind. Intuition is the spirit of the Source within. That is who you are. The intelligence within your heart is part of the whole intelligence. When you truly know this, you will have total freedom in life and see everyone and everything as the Source, with human conditioning. The intuition will be clear when you learn to embrace emotions and when you are awakened to true life intelligence. When you know all of this, you really will understand the light and the dark of life. You will have to be aware of your energy to protect yourself and not take on others energies. When you are awake, you will be more sensitive, but you will awaken to be authentic to your own energy also. This is when you will be living an almost perfect life. Life will knock you down, you will get tired, but it will not put you back.

You will ride the wave much quicker! You cannot be too serious about everything or you will always be trying to control thoughts and emotions and not experience peace and joy.

Do not be wondering what is going on in other people's minds or you will have no mind of your own. You will be living in the illusion of another person's mind. This is the way that people lose self-trust. Learn your own mind from a soul point of view. You will build your own self-trust and then live authentically in your own life and all other life.

Trust is the foundation of life.

Sliabh Bawn, Strokestown, County Roscommon.

Chapter 12

Mind

Your mind can be your own worst enemy. Nourish your mind and be the boss of your mind with the guidance of your own intuition. Keep yourself protected from who you let into your life; avoid gossiping, practice good self-talk and keep a clear conscience. Keep focusing on self-love in your heart and you will see love. Look at nature as romance, as that is what it is.

When you fall in love with the romance of nature, you will fall in love with the simple things in life. You will realize how amazing it is to be a part of this creation and experience it. You will not see anything detached. You will see everything as one. You will be independent. You will not be looking for security in others. You will feel safe in yourself, because you will know who you are. You will make the most of your time and invest in your own well-being every day. You will be free from conditioning to focus on who you really are. Focus more on the improvements in your life and they will manifest and acknowledge setbacks with awareness. They are very temporary and embrace setbacks as growth. We are all part of consciousness and when someone does something wrong, it can have an effect on us all, as we are one.

If someone does something good, it can have amazing benefits for us all as people, our home on planet earth and our Source, the creator and the universe. It is up to people of the world to make your life and everyone else's better and to treat earth as our precious home with respect. Keep this awareness every day and think of life as a short space of time. This amazing life we created is all based on love and anything bad anyone does, comes from fear. Remember we can only be loved-based or fear-based.

Medication of any sort is a temporary solution, the real solution is the intelligence within you; your spirit, The Source or your creator - whatever you believe that intelligence is to be. There is no denying it. It gives you life; do not disrespect it with chemicals to boost some rich man's ego, or your own ego.

Teach children gratitude or children will become spoiled adults, never happy and they will destroy their own life and everyone else's.

If you have witnessed bad breeding in dogs, you would not encourage more breeding of these dogs, unless something is wrong with you. It is the same with humans. Do not encourage looking up to some politicians who have no interest but to destroy lives to boost their own ego and some do not care about others. It is not normal for people to be handed everything by the state and have no gratitude. A lot of people do not want to take responsibility for themselves. People cannot have children at the drop of a hat and think everyone else has to pay for this child. This is disastrous for a child, to be brought up in this way of life. The people of the world created a mess with wars. There is no need whatsoever for this. People need to be taught early in life who they are, instead of half the people of the world becoming lost souls. I see people outside of courthouses thinking they are cool, but if they only knew how special they are, they would see how dumb their behavior.

I think all of the suffering in the world is waking a lot of people up to become soul-based and not ego-based.

Everything inside us and outside us affects our mind.

It is important to nourish our inner world and soul as it is important to nourish ourselves from our outer world, in balance of what is good for our minds.

Killashee, County Longford.

CHAPTER 13
Protecting Yourself

You have to be aware of people who do not live a conscious life; for example, a person who has a void in their life from being afraid or being controlled by a partner; or if they identify themselves only with a job or being manipulated at work. These are just a few examples. These people will try to force their void on people who are a soft touch or are close to them and let their boundaries down. Keep your self-respect and boundaries and do not allow anyone to use you or push their shortcomings onto you. Nobody in the world is better than anyone else, no matter who they are. We are all equal and we are all the one life force.

When a child is asking questions, it is important to answer them to educate them and to encourage their questions in life, so they will grow to investigate life for themselves. If they are not answered or respected correctly, they will be conditioned to become easily brainwashed and end up suffering trauma. Do not shame a child if misbehaving or doing anything wrong. Teach them about life and the quality of life.

Observe the way you see yourself, relationships, family, people you meet and the world. If you are constantly critical, it is your own life that needs looking at. You have to be aware and become an observer of self.

If someone speaks or acts towards you in a bad attitude, ask what is your own attitude to yourself. Do not disrespect yourself. Do not let a disrespectful person bring you down to their level. Keep practicing self-love and boundaries.

When you know yourself from within you are no longer mind-based. You become weightless by authentic self-living, without constantly examining yourself and others. You see everyone and everything with pure, unconditional love. You acknowledge yourself with love and oneness.

At the same time, you acknowledge that you are part of everyone and everything on earth and the universe, yet not attached and without expectations. You become happy and peaceful in the now and in the balance of life in the universe.

Spirit is breath, which is our life. Everything you need comes from your intuition. It is all at the source of who you are, to guide and teach you. It takes a certain awareness to understand. Breath is everything. When you truly understand this you will be a very strong, courageous person. You will realize how special you are. You will only live for the truth of self and others without relying on organisations, attachments and other people. You will be awake through the connection of the Source, the universe or whoever you believe that intelligence to be. You are not yourself or connected to the Source if you follow greed, ignorance, and some politicians that want to talk down to people and control people as if they own them. This is usually the behavior of spoiled children who are now adults or meant to be; or people who did not get enough attention, so they go for jobs where they can get attention. Whether it is correct or not they crave attention, not truth. Be aware always. Live true to self, because people watch a lot of rubbish on television from a young age, which is actually brainwashing people. If the person sitting in a chair only knew how special and how powerful they can be in their own lives, they would not let themselves be brainwashed by a box in the corner of the room.

A lot of people in the world have lives that are in chaos because of a lack of understanding and awareness to what their role in life is. For example, if parents do not know who they truly are, they will look for happiness in the child, which they only took part in bringing into the world. They do not own that child. However, they think that they do, so they try to distance from themselves by using the child. This alone can make a child codependent from a young age, which brainwashes the child into becoming codependent as an adult. This in turn creates guilt and shame in the child as an adult and their parents and causes trauma, which can have a domino effect to everyone. Awareness and understanding of who you are is so important to becoming a conscious adult.

Protect yourself with genuine people. Protect yourself. Be what you do and say in life. Do not get drawn into low energy conversations, gossip etc.

Protect your energy and you will protect your life.

Expression of intelligence in the force of nature.
Strokestown.

CHAPTER 14

Free will

Because we have free will, it is important to ask the universe whatever it is you want and not in a demanding and needy way. When you are ready, you will receive what is meant for you and your purpose in life at that moment in life.

If you do not get what you want, it is a blessing too. It is to teach you who you are first and that it is not all about fleeting pleasures. It is all for your sole purpose. Ask with conscious breathing, as the spirit is breath.

Anything you do not want in life, write on a piece of paper in a heartfelt way. Your sole purpose is to not become codependent and act in desperation. Soul growth is connected to the source. Write down any negative attachments about any negative people and energy around you on a piece of paper and burn it. See it going back to the universe to be taken care of. Let go of negative energy and move on with love.

You do not need a lot of good friends, just a few who are like-minded who you can trust.

Life is an amazing experience when you are connected to the Source with understanding and awareness; when you are free from conditioning and become your authentic self. Embrace the unknown and all the amazing opportunities to consciously experience and embrace this life and live your life purpose. Every one of us, past, present and future, are precious gifted souls. Be this gifted soul and do not waste your precious part in life's universe. Never forget who you are. You are an amazing part of the universe.

Do not attempt to find yourself with materialistic things. They are just things and money. These things are nothing special. You are the special one!

Do not be too keen in life, for example; do not give too much love away or your cup will be empty. Leave space to receive love.

By doing this, you will show you know yourself and that you have standards and boundaries and respect for self. Genuine people will then respect and love you. This goes for work and everything else in your life. You cannot write a letter or pray for everything, you have to know what you are about. Life is not a game and there is a reason for everything.

Letting go takes a lot of disciplined practice, to be aware of the ego, wanting to hold on to something that is not you - a person in your life or anything, because finding your purpose can be scary, until your emotions accept change. That is because some people have been through so much that they are afraid of failing again; but once you see the light it is so easy to get up again if you fall. Trust yourself and the process. Nothing will stop you, when you know how to get out of your head.

Even if you are not into listening to the star signs or astrology on YouTube as it doesn't resonate with you, they can teach you a lot about life. Reading is always good. It trains you to be present and educates you about life. Everyone's perception is different. It is up to yourself to investigate questions from childhood, especially if you need answers for yourself.

When we are living a life based on genuine love and not fleeting pleasures we have less resistance in our body, less stress, less negative emotion and more energy.

Fill your cells with love and joy and you, and other people around you, will have a lot less sickness.

All this rushing and racing in jobs is so pointless at the end of the day. It only creates sickness in some form.

Live your life to its fullest. You are your own boss.

Fakeness is trendy. Do not be a conformist. Be brave enough to be your authentic self. If you are not a deep person, you are only skimming the surface of life. You have to be spiritually awake to know who you are and to have lasting peace, joy and health.

There is an epidemic of children, teenagers and adults with mental health problems from constantly looking into the phone. More and more parents are telling me about this problem in families. Phones are man-made. Each human has amazing intelligence which is not man-made. Live from your soul, not mind conditioning.

It is time to protect earth, our home, for our children and generations to come. Do not mindlessly litter and destroy your home for your families in generations to come. You are poisoning their lives every day. Ignorance is the biggest problem in the world from not knowing the basics in life; right from wrong, love from hate and greed from generosity.

Change the course of direction in the world from fear to love. It is that simple, and your life and the people of the world will celebrate as one, because we are one.

Make that change today and every day. Do everything in the name of love. Do not take enemies personally. Lift everyone up and most importantly create an awareness to receive love. If you do not feel love, I for one, to whoever is reading this, wish you all the love in the world. Love is there all the time within, giving you life. You have it within yourself. You are special. Embrace life. You have the world in your hands. Make the most of it. Educate your kids about life; it will make their life so much better and yours in return. It is a person's responsibility to nourish roots in the child, not spoil them or neglect them. If you do not know this you should not have children. You have to know yourself first, only then will your life and your children and generations to come have a truly amazing life.

Keep it real and nourish your life with everything positive. Do not sell your soul cheaply to attachments, jobs or people. Embrace the amazing gift of life with the spirit of life's breath and be aware that you are a creation. Create the life of your dreams and live with a love for life. Embrace the journey of life.

Forest Park, Boyle, County Roscommon

CHAPTER 15

Elements

We are around 70% water, 12% earth, 6% air, 4% fire. We are the spiritual intelligence controlling the elements around us. It is important to nourish the elements within us. We connect to our creator through the elements and these elements create us. For us to know ourselves, meditation and shamanic drumming is good to connect with our creator and our ancestors. The spirit of our ancestors is in us all. There is good and bad conditioning in us from our ancestors. We are connected to our ancestors through elements, and spiritual meditation is important to live a life of purpose. We need to trust ourselves and trust in our ancestors. Trust in ourselves comes from knowing self.

If you do not know much about spiritual practice, it is important to read up on it first and be willing and open to learn. Visit spiritual teachers who are experienced instead of learning about it on YouTube. Do not become attached to the Internet. Instead become attached to nature, like a tree whose roots have grown deep and are firmly grounded. Then you will have authenticity to trust yourself and flourish. Take time to meditate looking at the trees which gives us fresh air to breathe. Imagine you are the tree. You are part of everything. You are all part of the intelligence force of life and it will bring awareness to who you are and your inner strength. Imagine you are all of nature around you. It will also bring awareness to your conditioning. Take a drive to different places to experience nature and feel the different energies. Always ask the arch-angel Michael to protect you beforehand from any negative energy and that you experience only good. See everyone and everything with love, because we are all one. You do not have to talk to anyone to see them as love. Keep peace nourished in your own life.

When your ego-mind is bothering you, remember that it is not just from conditioning from this lifetime, but also from thousands of years through our ancestors.

When you have the awareness of this, you will work on this by accepting it and seeing the divine being you are.

Sometimes observe the world as if you are a spirit, not only human. It will give you awareness to what people call, the simple things, which in fact are the Source, the creator, the universe and whatever you call the intelligence.

When you evolve to a high state of awareness and consciousness, you will tap into the source and your intuition. The more you get comfortable with your intuition, the more your life will grow for the better over time. You will less identify yourself with the ego-mind. You need to have a balanced life, enough rest, exercise, good food and have very little attachments to addictions like alcohol, smoking or coffee. Everything has to be balanced or your intuition will be distorted and your ego will create havoc.

There is no limit to the power of the mind. You can destroy your life or have an amazing life. If you destroy your own life, realize that if you are capable of destroying your life you are also capable of turning your life around and make it amazing. You are the creator. The human experience of life has its own down days. Surrender to this and embrace the lesson to keep you real.

When you are aware of the amazing creation you are, you become aware of life, and remind yourself of the importance of a sense of humor. Feed the humor and allow yourself to laugh often!

When you remind yourself of the billions of people who have passed through this human experience on earth in the last thousands, if not millions of years on the planet, is important to become aware of enjoying your short time here and not to worry about what people say or do. Enjoy life. Think of the word joy, and feel it every day and make that promise to yourself.

Be aware that you have an inner child within which holds the positive and negative effects from your upbringing. Discern which are false beliefs, lack of love, basic respect from others and self-worth. Any issues in adult life mostly come from childhood. Investigate your own life in depth. Heal, love and protect that inner child and respect others. Nobody is above anyone else, no matter how much somebody thinks they are. If they do, then they are foolish. None of us are perfect. We are a perfect creation having a human experience.

Be aware where your thoughts come from and if they are human conditioning. This will tell you what is real and what is not.

Your divine experiences are enough. Pleasures are an extra. Do not be codependent on pleasure. That a lot of people's downfall. Their desires get out of control and become needy. They spiral out of control until the suffering wakes them up. There is sometimes a reason for suffering as it can bring people back to their senses to teach them who they are.

Happiness cannot be bought. It is a natural state, when you know who you are. Fake has been the trend for a long time. Sometimes you have to let go of people in your life and anyone who is draining your energy by being ego-based, cut them out of your life. It is amazing how quickly your life will improve. You do not owe anyone anything by taking on their drama. Own your life and you will mature into the purpose of your being. You are not a conformist.

You can truly only live in your own shoes; nobody else's. A job does not own you either. That is why it is called a job.

There are some people who make a lot of money out of fakeness. It is a superficial life. It is better to have a real life.

When you come into contact with people, see them with love - because it is the same source of life that is in them, that is in you. We have all been conditioned by human experience and we all have our own purpose in life. When a person is not nice, see it just as conditioning and a defense mechanism that a lot of the time both parties are unconscious to.

Surrender to the process when going through a tough time. Know it is part of your process. Surrender to trying to control the process. Surrender to letting go. Letting go is practicing itself. Most importantly, surrender to old habits of negative feelings which you gathered in tough times. Surrender to embracing the new you with unlimited possibilities.

Any problems are embedded in the subconscious mind. You are not the mind. You are consciousness. Every person you meet has a subconscious mind which is conditioned differently.

Know that this is just the mind, so do not take negativity towards you too seriously. See people as a source and expression of the Source, or creator. When you genuinely know this, you will have peace and love in life.

If you are in the habit of always thinking of what is going wrong, change it to what could go right instead. Look at the amazing intelligence in water to produce so much life; when the example of this proof of source sinks in, it will bring you to your true senses. Be aware that emotions are important for love and in knowing right and wrong. When you are living consciously you are living from the heart, so it is important to keep a balance in life. If not, you could get triggered to react before you even think about negative situations. Just like when you live a true authentic life, the feeling of love flows, without you even thinking about it.

Also be aware adults that are childlike are authentic, but are not mature enough for relationships or responsibilities. They have very limited knowledge of life. They will identify themselves with a job title for example. Childlike adults are people that never investigated their own life and tend to be conformists and jealous types. They are one of the most dangerous of people. They will give you their trust while planning to manipulate you. A lot of businesses are manipulating people. One man working for an international company told me he was manipulated into working fourteen days in a row, plus overtime in the evenings, for little or no extra money, because they gave him the title of a supervisor. On his first day off after fourteen days work in a row, they were constantly ringing his private number. I was talking to this man because the stress and pressure in his life from the company wore him down and made him feel not worthy. They took control of his life. His children and wife were feeling neglected. This can have a devastating effect on families and children when they grow up. National and international companies are using tactics to manipulate and brainwash staff in the name of greed. Sometimes in life you have to step out of your comfort zone of being nice and cut negative people or jobs out of your life, that do not meet your standards.

As people, cities, towns and villages become more modern, people's perception of who they are and what their life is about can change. People change to be more mind-based, identifying themselves with things like houses and cars. They have lost touch with nature and the earth that feeds us.

I think one of the reasons more and more people have dogs is because these pets have not changed like humans. It is a reminder to humans that our natural state is unconditional love. Like music, pets are a great quick reminder of love. Without love we are weak.

A problem in the world is that too many people believe life is all about *I*. We are all in this life together. We come from the one source and we live from the one source which created air, soil, fire and water. All sorts of life come from source and people have to respect this. Know all this greed and running and racing to things is getting to people. These people live a false identity. Respect the gift of life. Listen to your intuition and not the conditioned mind.

When a person is suffering, during the suffering or afterwards it is important not to constantly identify yourself with the sufferings. It had its reason and purpose. Do not let yourself believe or feel that you have to suffer in life, when you only have to have balance in life. You can enjoy life. Remind yourself of the feeling of enjoying life, like the child that is not aware of how tough life can be. That inner child is in everyone. Nourish your inner child and protect it. Live the feeling of inner joy like a child. Live with unconditional love from the heart, without fear. See yourself wild and free like nature and in harmony.

In my opinion, our creator created winter and summer, because otherwise humans would destroy the soil and earth altogether. In short winter nights we should rest and have lots of family time, which is important for the well-being of people in every way. Greed and stupidity is destroying lives and families. Every day we see so much suicide and crime in the world. This is the price we pay for some politician's greed and power. Because of all of this, when you become awake to whom you really are, do not try and change the world by yourself. People who try to change everyone, end up exhausted in every way and back to feeling lost. This need to change everyone is controlling and comes from codependency. Both come from childhood. Live your own life to its fullest. You cannot change anyone. It is up to people to change themselves when their own timing is correct. Some people never wake up to who they really are because their conditioning is too deep, and they are afraid to examine or take responsibility for their own life.

They either surround themselves with unconscious people like themselves, or join some organization of fake people who get defensive if anyone says the truth. If this is you, investigate your own life for yourself, not an organization for advice. There are too many people asleep in the world and most of the time those who run organisations are brainwashed. You need to have an attitude like a lion to have belief in yourself. Believe in yourself and you will be your own strength, not on an organization which will make you weak.

Some people want to know everyone else's business; this is a perfect example of a person who cannot mind their *own* issues in life and are not exposed to life or the world around them. Have nothing to do with these people. When you get to know the source from within mother earth and the universe, you are unlimited in that state of consciousness. You can reach this state of consciousness through meditation and drumming. If you are in an advanced stage of consciousness you can meet spiritual guides, and get advice from ancestors on staying balanced, or advice for yourself in any way. Shamanic people go back thousands of years to pre-Christian times. There are more and more people going back to the Shamanic way of life and connecting with the source through nature where we came from. It is best to learn from experienced shamanic practitioners.

Like everything in life, you get people that jump on the bandwagon thinking they know it all. It is like some people coming out of college brainwashed that they know everything with all of these degrees.

If you are in an environment that goes against the law of nature, it breaks the spirit of who you are. That is why it takes so long to heal.

There are lots of people in the world who have an illusion that they own you or have authority over you. This could be in your relationships, employer or government. Nobody owns you and you do not own anyone. Stand in your own shoes and live your own unique life. That is where your power is. Conformists are weak. Be yourself.

Your enemies could turn you into your *own* worst enemy. Do not let anyone push their problems onto you. Stand strong and firm to the truth and set yourself free. After every encounter you have to step out of your comfort zone.

This can take time, because you have to get used to resistance and accept that some people choose to live a fake life. If you are the person pushing your problems onto everyone else, it will catch up with you. Nobody gets away with going against the law of the universe and nature.

See yourself, everyone and everything with love and light. We are the elements, the earth, air, water and fire. The spirit is in each element.

It is important for us to have awareness of the elements and to nurture ourselves with the elements in nature every day. The spirit of our creator and also our ancestors is in us. There is both bad and good in us from our ancestors. Through Shamanic drumming and meditation we learn the Ying and Yang of ourselves and allow healing and growth, to be in line with our creator.

Drumshanbo, County Leitrim

Sliabh Bawn, Strokestown, County Roscommon

CHAPTER 16

Freedom

Freedom from authority is very important to live authentically. When you become aware of what freedom is, you will not let anyone or anything hold you back from living. Most people are just existing and not living. Do not be codependent on people or jobs. A job is important and it is important to interact with people. You will only have true joy and happiness when you have freedom.

We all live in this world, but each person lives in their own world. No two people can see the world the same. How cool is that? There is also the spirit world.

Sometimes you have to have the masculine attitude of life integrated in a very nice way with the feminine energy. Sometimes when you evolve enough, you will authentically enjoy the slog of life when it happens. Learn to enjoy the unpleasant as much as the pleasant. Become attached to nothing or anyone, in a state of flow with light and dark. It is an amazing experience. This is life. Every day, let your bare feet touch the earth and it will nourish you and keep your thoughts and feelings grounded.

Look at nature for a few minutes every morning in all of its creation; it will give you the perfect start to the day!

I am far from perfect and I happy about that. Imagine how boring life would be if everything was perfect?

Be aware of anticipation for what it is and do not mix it up with intuition. When anticipation happens, remind yourself with a bold attitude that we are here for a short time and we are going to make the most of this life.

A holiday or day trips away from where you live are important for expanding the mind. It reminds you that you are important and how important fun is.

Holidays and short breaks away are also good for changing your perception about an issue or a problem.

There is the heart and the gut type people. The heart type people suffer more than even love-based, because of so much fakeness around them in the world. They are the purest people and most true to themselves, everyone and everything. Their pureness brings on more suffering and when they process this suffering, nothing can stop a heart-based person who has awareness and wisdom. When you are really high in spirit, be aware of coming down in human energy. Try to keep being fun and loving in everyday life. It will make the come down easier.

Make sure every time you release negative energy to replace it with positive energy.

When you are awake to the spiritual aspect of life, it is important not to forget the human aspect of life. Embrace all aspects of life, because all are equally important.

Adults continue to look for love all the time from outside us, because they never learned to love themselves from within. To be real in every way and have happiness, we need to have general love for ourselves from within, but not with an ego-based love. When we do not love from within, we are in fear of rejection and of not being good enough. There is no easy or quick way to learn self-love. It takes years to learn and enjoy the journey. The down and the ups are an important part of the journey also. Take responsibility in observing your thoughts, emotions and actions. Stepping out of your comfort zone is one of the most powerful things you can do. Do not worry. It is scary for everyone, especially at the start. Embrace this rollercoaster! Change your perception. You will be surprised that when you dig deep into your spirit; the source of who you are will show itself. The spirit, the Source, creation, your ancestors and everything in the universe is within. Dig deep. Lose the conditioning of fear and reveal your true spirit.

There are a lot of people in the world afraid to live and they are easily manipulated into fear of death. Our body is like a vessel. Look how big the ship is, but look at the spirit of creation that carries the vessel.

We are much larger in spirit than the human experience. Death is the loss of the vessel, not the spirit. We have nothing to fear in death. In this life experience our human body carries our spirit. Look after your spirit.

Tarmonbarry, County Roscommon

CHAPTER 17
Loneliness and Lockdowns

If you are in a job where you spend long periods of time on your own, this can be devastating to you in every way. It is important to have the spirit of another human being in your company for a few hours a day at least, even if you and other person don't see eye-to-eye. Seeing eye-to-eye with another person is one portion of life. The presence of the spirit of another human in your life is so much more than any conditioning. It is a beating heart. The presence of a beating heart is special.

Never be afraid to love yourself. Have a genuine love with awareness of the Source within you and around you. Remember, there is only one of you in the world. Appreciate how special you are. You were created by the Source.

Do not forgive and forget too quickly. Give everyone and everything a second chance. Take your time looking for the truth and trust that it will reveal itself. Do not fall for false trust. When you only live from truth and respect you will be respected, and you will have firm boundaries.

Imagination is your tool to success in any aspect of life. The imagination has to be from consciousness or good ego.

If there were no other people in the world, or very few people in the world, we would not know how to experience life on this earth.

Be moved by life, and move yourself and the people around you for the better in truth.

Value your relationship with the Divine, for it is sacred.

Be the awareness that is giving you the gift of breath, eyesight, hearing, taste, touch, smell and intelligence to life within you and around you; the intelligence inside you that created your heart, all the organs, nervous system, skin and every part of you. You have to live with this awareness to be your own person in line with the intelligence of your creator. For self-trust, love, peace, health, happiness and intuition, this is how you listen to your creator who guides you on your everyday journey of life. Practice self-respect, love and care in every way. Appreciate nature. It is the creator's creation for us to live in, to nourish us and to teach us. In return we need to nourish the home which the creator entrusted to us.

It is important to practice meditation for a time every day that suits you. Some people need more stillness than others. It could be prayer, music, etc.

Another important thing to do from time to time is give yourself awareness of the billions of people in the world that look at you as just another of the billions. You will realize then that you are not important, no matter your wealth or anything you have in life. Then your troubles and worries become very small. They are not important at all.

Tarmonbarry, County Roscommon

CHAPTER 18

Awake

When we are awake to the amazing creation we are, we become aware of the intelligence that created us. We live by intuition which directs us. Listen to your own intuition and not what everyone else is thinking.

This is a very mind-based world because of money and importance placed on status. You are more important than the politics of life. You are a special edition of creation.

It is nice to practice emptying from society, emptying from thoughts, feelings, people, attachments and everything. Feed the deep feeling of freedom. Sit with this practice of freedom every morning. Then in the mind's eye re-emerge into society unattached to anything and take part in society in a loving, caring way with the feelings of freedom.

Virtual living, social media and a fast-paced lifestyle are part of the modern world. It takes too much of our attention from ourselves and we give too much time concentrating on other people and material things and comparing ourselves with everyone else unconsciously. Because we are living so fast, we are seldom living as who we are in the present. The main problem with this is we live off everyone else's opinions and usually the negative. We are living too fast to know ourselves. It is the same with most people, so it is a vicious cycle. We have to be our own person. Other people's way of living, talking, behavior and what they say or do, is absolutely none of our business, even if it is directed at us.

An exception to this is being bullied. There are a lot of sick people who think it is normal to bully, harass and use people. This is the product of a society with a bad upbringing.

Imagine you witnessed an apparition and how amazing that would be. You are the living version of that apparition you experienced.

You come from and are that spiritual source. You are the spirit of Source – or whoever you believe your Source to be.

The wildness of nature feeds our soul with a wildness to feel alive and to feel free and at one with the Source and ourselves.

You have to learn the spiritual love of the Source to feel love for yourself, everyone else, earth, all that is true, love, peace and confidence. Celebrate the love of your own creation. All creation brings joy and harmony to life and peace into the world. Spiritual love is being grateful for the Source that created you and gives you life. You do not take life. It is given to you with love. Be grateful for the love of the Source's creation.

People do not realize that they are losing their way. They are captured in a mind-based world of thinking and feeling.

Embrace your individuality to be conscious of how special you are. There is just one of you.

If a person does not have empathy, there is no limit to the destruction they can do to people and society.

Trust your own power. When you learn to trust your own power within and when you get to know that power, you are an amazing force of nature. You can do or be anything you want, in a natural way. This power will never collapse. It is not ego. Ego power is fleeting.

Learn the true voice/feeling/third eye within that is in harmony with Source. Nourish your energy while you can with sleep and work. Resting is important. Creative resting, good food and good people are important, as is good company. Do not replace this with cats or dogs. They are important, but people are more important. Do not put all your own love into pets, other people, a job or things. Spend time in exercise, listening to music and nice sounds; anything that nourishes the soul.

CHAPTER 19

Healing

The purpose of Spiritual Energy Healing is to bring people in contact with their soul and purpose in life; spiritually, mentally, emotionally and physically.

I will start by writing first why energy healing is important.

A lot of people are losing touch with themselves more and more. Modern life has simply become too fast for us. We commute long distances to work. We eat 'on the go' from deli counters; we drink too much coffee which only brings quick stints of pleasure - not the energy people unconsciously think it is giving them. In fact it actually does more harm in many ways.

Many people are under heavy workloads; forced into shift work, working long hours to cover bills, mortgages etc. With cuts in wages and increases in bills, people are feeling the pressure and some have turned to drinking at home. They haven't money to go to places for social gatherings such as pubs or restaurants. This is bad for people. Social life is an outlet to nourish the soul. It is important to interact with people socially and not behind the screen of a phone or computer. Often, in this way, people get the wrong opinion of themselves. They judge themselves by messages they take up wrongly, from people they don't really know. This creates all sorts of problems mentally and emotionally.

There are more people looking after themselves physically which is good, but some of these people act like it is both pleasure and pain. They are also trying to fit exercise in a short space of time which turns the exercise into a chore, causing more imbalances in their life.

People don't have the time for proper family life. Parents are often too busy to nurture themselves. Some of this is their own doing, by building big houses or buying cars they can't afford. I put this down to ego.

They are more interested in living off other people's opinions, when instead they should be educating themselves, looking for the answers in their heart and living from their soul.

Children are too busy looking into phones and are not being not taught the basics in life; for example, love from hate, greed from generosity and right from wrong.

Some people are turning to drink and drugs to balance emotions. Some of these, or all of these people, are sensitive and are not told they are having a spiritual awakening. They are becoming conscious of their own emotions; mentally and spiritually. A lot of these people are very intelligent and creative. They are aware of love, fear, good and bad, and they have to balance their human experience when they are spiritual. Instead they are labeled with depression, which is a feeling within their spiritual experience, just like happiness is a feeling. These are just feelings, not labels.

Some people identify themselves with their job, house, car, religion, exercise, food, farming, money, etc.

You have to be aware that negative people do not like positive people. If you are in company with negative people for long enough, they will drag you down with them. You have to take responsibility for yourself, that you are not the negative one and talking to people in a correct tone of voice. If you are in a negative situation for long periods at home or work, you have to watch your own stubbornness and take action to leave or do something about the situation. Life is too short!

Sometimes problems for people or family can go back generations. From the day we are born, we are all learning. There is no perfect life. We are spiritual beings having a human experience. I think it is very important to know we are having a spiritual experience for us to understand ourselves; to have faith in our higher source of intelligence, and to know there is life after death, just as there was life before us.

Spiritual energy healing goes back thousands of years.

People sometimes think the easiest way to peace and happiness is outside of themselves, but is only found in the soul. There are more people turning to energy healing, because it is turning people's lives around for the better.

It has turned my life around to great understanding, awareness, peace, and most importantly of all, love for myself. It is very important to truly love yourself, not in an ego based way, and allow for off days. That is life, when people learn and grow. They are laying the groundwork for peace and love and creativity and connecting to their soul.

There are seven chakras in energy healing:

1. 7th is the crown chakra- spirituality
2. 6th is the third eye chakra - awareness
3. 5th is the throat chakra - communication
4. 4th is the heart chakra - love and healing
5. 3rd is the solar plexus chakra - wisdom and power
6. 2nd is the sacral chakra - sexuality and creativity
7. 1st is the root chakra - basic trust

If any of these chakras are out of balance due to some of the reasons I mentioned already, you can have all sorts of problems; for example, feelings of depression, anxiety, mental problems, spiritual and physical problems. Feelings are not labels.

Energy healing works by getting to root of the problems - taking away the most recent problem and the next one after that, until you notice the improvement after a healing session. You notice the improvement every day and if you have an odd bad day that is okay. This is the first sign that you are getting better. It is just that your old problems are a reminder, but bad days will get less frequent over time and disappear eventually. It depends on the person and how long you have had the problem.

Energy healing turns your life around over a short period. If the person had a problem for forty years, within a year of energy healing and therapy, they will have turned their life around. You will feel a lot better in yourself and with others. You will be at peace in your life. There are no politics in energy healing. Healing people are big hearted people. They have been through it all themselves. Healing people are passionate about helping others. They have no interest in shallow quick fixes. Energy healing takes out the bad and plants the seed of love and peace, and nourishes that seed until it blooms!

Sometimes people have to go through a journey of fear for a period of time, to change them from being unconscious to conscious

People are returning to the Spiritual Source of life and natural healing because it is true and natural and from the heart, the source of all creation. Energy healing brings balance back into people's lives and when all the chakras are in balance, the person is balanced in every way. When chakras are blocked or not balanced, emotions run high and the negative ego tends to control the mind. When the chakras are balanced we have to keep nurturing ourselves in every way. The correct job must suit the person. This could include the correct working hours, what food you eat, enough sleep, exercise, having correct thoughts and learning how to change thoughts and feelings. If they are not correct and you do not love yourself, or keep practicing self-love and have a good foundation in yourself, then you will revert back to old ways. You have to be diplomatic and earn respect. This is shown by the tone of your voice, enjoying your own company and that of others and not trying to control situations. Let life be as it is, in any situation.

Be aware that everyone is on their own journey in life. I have to stress *their own* journey in life, because sometimes we wonder why people can't see certain ways if their life is not correct; like living to work and identifying themselves by their job for instance. Sometimes people are not ready to wake up and really experience life. The pain of learning so much in a short space of time would be too much for them to cope with. Their own journey means being independent, being responsible for the love they give themselves and others, knowing when a person has to stand their own ground. They have to have no respect for themselves, because someone is not respecting them. They are projecting their problems onto you and everyone else, and this will bring low energy.

Energy healing is a divine source from a higher consciousness. When you are trained and nurtured enough in energy healing you can naturally feel healing. You can sense and feel the light which is the spirit of the source. You can feel that healing is present and taking place in you as a spiritual teacher/healer. The client will be guided from higher consciousness through the spiritual teacher/healer.

When the chakras are cleansing and clearing you will deal with negative emotional baggage, and negative ego, which will then change overtime with healing, to positive emotions and a positive ego. You will change from a low energy, to a high energy. Higher energy is in the top half of the body. You will feel highly light with the flow of life, by not dwelling on the negative, but only positive thoughts.

Remember when you went through a difficult time that blessings came from the very tough times. It is a genuine and long lasting love and peace. When you were not happy, you were caught up in your own idea of reality. When your chakras are cleared and operating correctly you are conscious, and when you have an off day in your heart, see it as a spiritual practice. All this knowledge and wisdom comes from a higher consciousness. That is where the healing higher energy comes from.

As humans we are all energy with our voice, thoughts, movement, etc. Everything in the world is created by energy and energy has to be healed and nourished, like everything else. The only way to do this is by healing from the Source. From my point of view as a spiritual teacher/healer, it is difficult to express fully what the limit of energy healing is. It is a knowing from deep within the universe and my heart of love and peace and at the same time understanding a human experience. That is why it is important to know about our spiritual experience and fall in love with it, because that is where love comes from. Love is a positive energy that needs nourishment, sometimes for ourselves and for spiritual teachers/healers in healing our client.

Sometimes love is only a word to some people. They have to go through hardship or a spiritual awakening to understand what love really is. Love is a feeling from the heart and a higher consciousness, but to maintain that love we have to learn a lot about life.

Energy healing connects us to our Source. There are no politics about what religion is correct, or who or what way of thinking is correct. We are humans and I think about 20% of people in the world are conscious, and it is our job to spread the love as spiritual teachers/healers. We should spread this love unconditionally when we give healing. The healing is directly from our Source to our client.

Some clients will not see results for a while because they have so much to process in their lives to learn and grow, to go from negative energy to positive, and to become a higher conscious, from fear based to love based.

I read one time that nature's gift is stillness. Stillness is calm, with positive emotions and ego allowing us to step into the light. It takes time, patience and practice in every way. Look at the wind blowing the trees and the energy it has. The tree shakes around although well rooted in the ground, it stands firm and is nourished. It is rooted in the ground and grows tall and produces leaves through energy, and cleans the air. Just like we nourish and grow to produce love and life.

Like energy, healing is life force energy. Everyone in the world is an amazing gift, and the world and nature and the universe is a gift from the Source. Everyone should look within themselves and spread love unconditionally, practice self growth, bring up your energy and lift up your spirits. Try some energy healings if you need a change in your life. It will plant the seed like the flower and you will blossom! We bring up our energy by feelings. Take responsibility for yourself and your feelings, and at the same time do not take life too seriously or personally. Go with the flow of life's energy force.

When we are critical of ourselves and others that is a lower energy trying to control life – trying to control what people say and do by controlling situations. It is important to trust in ourselves and to go with the flow of life. Try not to give attention to the negative. Understand that it is teaching you to be yourself.

Spiritual healing creates space in a person's inner world, which allows room for awareness of consciousness and space from distractions and conditioning of a person's outer world.

What is a spiritual teacher/healer?

A spiritual teacher/healer is someone who feels and sees life from a cellular soul level. This is where our spiritual source is. A person connected on a soul level is connected to the spirit. This is where a spiritual teacher/healer receives gifts from sometimes. The best spiritual teachers/healers suffered trauma in their own lives. This trauma brought them to their deep connection of Source.

Everyone is a soul created by a spirit. Some people are not connected to their Source due to human conditioning. This book teaches people that suffering in life is because their soul wants them to connect to their spiritual self, for their higher good.

Healing is called energy healing, because everything is energy. There is energy in your body, your voice, the earth, air, water and the sun.

Kilglass, Rooskey, County Roscommon

CHAPTER 20

Sound Healing

Sound healing is one of the best forms of healing. It lifts your energy and creates good vibration instantly in line with the universe. There are a lot of distorted frequencies on television and radio. It is good to heal and neutralize your soul with healing frequencies like quality music, mantras and upbeat music. Either the tone or the lyrics can nourish the soul. If you feel down and are not sure of the reason, you might have picked up on someone else's negative energy. When you become awake, you become sensitive to energy. Use sage on yourself and your home. Ask your spirit guides and angels to take away any negative energy. Ground yourself with bare feet on the floor, or outside in nature is better.

Life is far from perfect, because of this human experience in this generation and all generations before us. Our parents were brainwashed to believe that everything we need is on the outside of us, when everything we need is on the inside of us. If you can realize the reason for suffering, you will begin to find yourself from within. You will not find your identity in a car or blocks of a house. They are false identities. The Source isn't just outside you; the spirit of the Source *is* you.

We are all one, so treat others the way that you should treat yourself. The only separation is body and conditioning. When you see someone on the street sleeping rough, an alcoholic, or drug addict; remember these people are probably more aware of the injustice and fear in the world, caused by some people in powerful positions, or unconscious people.

Some of these people become aware of the injustice in world too young and are not mature enough to handle it. Some people just do not know who they are because they were not mentally and emotionally educated correctly by parents, who were not correctly educated either; they either got too much attention or not enough and received no discipline in life.

They believe they can do whatever they want and speak to anyone without respect and that everyone else is supposed to pick up the pieces. Parents feel guilty that their off-spring are acting like children at thirty or forty years of age. These children can put a guilt trip on the parent to continue to bathe them in happiness, while both parents and their sons and daughters throw their souls away. They try to avoid themselves or express themselves with anger and jealousy. These people crave love and healing from others in relationships but often repeat cycles of blaming everyone else.

True love is very rare, because most people do not love themselves from within. Most people marry and they do not know why. Sometimes they marry because they are codependent or because other people are getting married and they want to tick that box also. Others marry to have more control over the other person as they think they own the other person. Some get married so they can live off other people's opinions. It is perfectly okay to be married or single, when you know who you are and what your words and actions are in life. It is perfectly okay to be single and look for love and not romance; once you are clear of your wants to the other person, and the other person understands and is not codependent or has ideas about controlling your life. Marriage is good if you do not believe you own the other person and you are both evolved enough to know who you are, and you are not getting married because of man-made ideas.

It is important to be aware of your energy and how you manage it, where your focus, attention, energy and balance are. If you are in a job where you use your head a lot like in an office, or if you are driving and are sitting down a lot of time, it is important to balance this energy and get exercise - not just for the physical health, but by exercise you are bringing energy from the head to the body, hands and feet. We are not meant to be sitting for such long periods. It is important to work to feel alive and to have a purpose. If you do not work for some reason, try working with nature outside, like gardening or some other activity.

If you cannot go outside, have some indoor hobbies. We are not meant to be sitting down with nothing to do every day, with too much time to think. It does not suit most people, as you may know yourself very well. Boredom can creep in and that is when negative thoughts and emotions manifest.

Strokestown House

CHAPTER 21

Space

Everything is not as intense as we think; there is always space.

Space between people at all times.

Space in our body. In nature. For example, if you are in an accident everything seems in slow motion. This is the Source. Nature especially produces space in areas out of our control. This is why it is important to try to live authentically, because if we try to control space in our lives, we are trying to control everything in life and its natural process. One thing to be curious of is our breath when going through tough times. It regulates the nervous system in life.

Space in nature. Space between earth and sky. Space between night and day. Space within. Space in time. Space in relationships.

Space is an important part of life. Space between waves is as nice as the wave when observed.

Space to make decisions.

See yourself and everyone as the beating heart. That is what we are – a beating heart.

Life force has a momentum and sometimes we need to slow down or speed up to suit that momentum – for instance, if we feel we are slipping back into the past, we might need to speed up life by keeping busy, getting out and enjoying ourselves; or maybe we are meant to sit with a situation and slow down and observe to see it for what it is. That is it.

Remember to feel light not heavy.

Sometimes people use anger to control people. Anger comes from fear.

Take your shoes off. Put them in the middle of the floor. Spend time looking at your empty shoes, thinking what way do you want to see yourself in those shoes.

Sometimes in life we have to create the correct space in our lives to investigate life, so we can move forward. An example of this is; it takes a woman and a man to make a baby so we all have both feminine and masculine energy.

Some people are born more feminine or more masculine. These people are usually very nice people because they have investigated their own life from a young age. They have great acceptance of life. These people live from their soul creation.

The feminine and masculine out of balance from human conditioning is different. It is because of people not living ladylike and gentlemanlike. Society and modern world is so fast that people can become lost souls. It can break people's spirit and make people weak, become defensive, go on petty power trips, cause manipulating and controlling behavior. We are energy and energy is fast. We all have to work at keeping our feminine and masculine energy in balance.

To be ladies and gentlemen, we need space for awareness to understand and move forward in life.

A woman is a portal between the spiritual and human aspect of life. Because of this a woman sometimes matures quicker than men.

If you are insecure about speaking – look at the amazing gift of voice you have. Use it for truth, better love, boundaries and your purpose in life.

The earth and the universe create every day.

We create great lives – not destroy.

Anyone who is obnoxious towards you is coming from fear. They are at a very low vibration. Rise above it and see them for where they are in life without judgment, and you will have understanding to stay in a high vibration.

Live every day appreciating the special amazing creation that planet earth, you and everyone is.

Coynes Cottage, Tourmakeady, County Mayo

Chapter 22

Nervous System

An important part of our own spiritual journey is getting to know ourselves. Boundaries, food, exercise, social life, hobbies and rest are all important. We need to nourish, protect, strengthen and trust our nervous system too. Our nervous system is our guide and compass for our emotional mental wellbeing in life.

We cannot abuse our nervous system by suppressing it with drink or drugs, working too hard, being addicted to food or exercise. Everything has to be in balance. If we keep abusing our nervous system when it is working to help us, we will not learn deeply what is right or wrong and face growth, no matter how painful it is. Any habit we pick up, even if it is a bad habit, is a withdrawal from our nervous system like giving up smoking. Our system thinks it needs to smoke because it was conditioned to believe that it needs to smoke; to calm nervous energy by distraction and addictive ingredients, which in turn cause more anxiety.

And at same time it is not all about giving up something.

A lot of time nervousness should be embraced as something good. All creation flows through the nervous system which is who we are on a cellular level. This is our creation of source deep within us. It is here. All creation comes from life, art, music, voice and painting. Anything coming from our good nervous system is divine intelligence and all else falls into place.

For anyone suffering from their nerves and trust in self.

When you are captured by the emotion of fear, it is not possible most of the time to have self-trust or trust in most people, except for a good therapist or social care worker who builds up trust with you, such as physiatrists' etc.

Fear is and can be the most devastating thing/emotion in life.

It actually is a feeling your life is under threat, so we have to learn to create a visual and energy space between people and crowded places. We have to do this in a conscious way. Words can make you feel emotional and cause mental fear. This can cause sickness and maybe death. Read self-help books, get therapy, eat correct food, drink more water, have little caffeine and go out in nature and exercise. Go out in public and allow yourself to be nervous; no matter how hard it is.

If you feel fear, that is okay. Do not beat yourself up. It is your business and nobody else's how you feel. The more you put yourself out in society the more you will build your own self-trust. You have to be a bit wild from within to express yourself for who you really are and to experience the freedom of life. Just like nature is free, we should be free. Those who rely on drugs, or money, or greed are weak. They are in some way trying to fill a void. Everyone is so special. Appreciating the beauty of nature and embracing who we really are can fill the voids in life.

Embrace your nervous system. Having a perception of your nervous system is of key importance. It is your teacher. Even though sometimes it seems to be far from your best friend, it is. Without it you would not evolve to being the special person that you are. If you feel nervous, change your perception to feeling excited from a soul point of view. Some people *feel* life, where others just *think* life.

Some are nervous and because they do not feel life so much, they are not impacted by nervousness. If you are a deeply creative person, it is normal to feel nervous sometimes. Don't beat yourself up about it.

CHAPTER 23

Knowing Thyself

Years ago it was more of a natural life. Even if people were not spiritually awake they were in nature more and had time to spend in it. Nature nourishes the soul and who we are.

Today more people are becoming spiritually awake, usually through suffering, because of a void created by ego in society and human conditioning. There is a lot of greatness in the modern world. We have all comforts but these have come at a price, where people are identifying themselves by worldly things and image instead of the amazing creation they are. Most of the world has become a culture of false living. This is why there is so much chaos in the world. The modern world created a lack of trust in knowing who you are. People have become dangerous to themselves and each other. People lost their voice and society is breaking down. People feel a need to start all over again and they really are.

Be the art of life. A true life is a natural art expression. It is time to step out of programmed minds.

Words are made of energy. Like all life, everything is energy. This is why words have so much power.

Exercise helps us through the spiritual and human aspects of life.

A spiritual teacher/healer is someone who heals without passing on past trauma, because they are free from all conditioning.

A wounded spiritual teacher/healer is a person who is still carrying trauma and can pass trauma on without knowing it. They could be a narcissist, or someone who was totally spoiled which caused their trauma. This person learns a lot about healing but never let's go of their past and passes it on to others because they are brainwashed into believing 'it's all about me'.

Strokestown House & Gardens, Roscommon

CHAPTER 24

Our Limited Minds

Why do we have limited minds? Some of us more than others and what can we do about it? First it is natural part of our perception, to keep us in our comfort zone; to feel we are protecting ourselves which is correct for us, but too long in our comfort zone sometimes is doing us more harm than good. It is important at times to step out of our comfort zone to fulfill our purpose in life, and very importantly to inspire our children and families to know how to make changes in life as we mature, with awareness and understanding.

This is important for our own life, family and the generations to come and society in general. Whenever we see obstacles - which could be through thought, feelings, a job, something in society - with awareness and understanding your life will flourish. You are a Divine Creator. By changing your conditioning, thought, perceptions and feelings, you will over time become true to your soul's purpose and not be ruled by an egoist mind. You will be much happier and healthier. You will have better relationships, job, become part of a better society and world.

When a limited, egoist mind is changed to a life of pureness, based on ones' own true purpose and not a limited conditioning, controlled person/society/world - you have become yourself. We all have to be aware of limits and their teachings. Awareness of the wildness of nature while out in nature nourishes our natural freedom from any limits within us and around us. Humans control nature sometimes by abusing nature. This in turn is destroying our home, our provider - earth. Control of all life is destruction. We need a certain amount of freedom to be in harmony with all life but not to poison our water, soil and air. There has to be major change to how nature is treated. We desperately need to plant a lot of trees to compensate for this modern world and its climate.

Another form of limited life is the phrase 'larger than life; for example, no human being can make blood, a heart, or eyes; therefore our spiritual intelligence is unlimited compared to the human aspect. When we are babies and children growing up, we are full of joy, love and excitement. We are naturally close to our spiritual creation. As we get older we naturally mature into adulthood. We in turn teach our children the basics of love, generosity and respect through guidance. If they are not taught these basics they will look for attention in the wrong ways, so by the time they are adults their life is upside down. The evidence is all over society. Life can become rough, tough and too serious with all that is going on in the world.

To be aware of the amazing spiritual intelligence you and everyone on earth is, remember back to when you were a child living without all the conditions - that inner child is in everyone - just like the life of our ancestors is in us. It is important to nourish your own and others inner child.

Be careful, as some people are so damaged from conditioning that they want pass it on to whoever comes near them. They are also very protective of their space. Do not patronize or speak ill about these people, understanding is needed, but keep boundaries.

There is only so much everyone can do and everyone's life is their own business. We need to be aware and acknowledge this. Do not sell your self-worth by looking for approval.

For a person with a good balance in life, it is still perfectly normal to feel up and down. The morning, midday, evening and night all have different energy feelings. We must live at the same phase as these changing time energies. Sometimes we have to be fragile with life and sometimes we have to be like a rebel, by being free and strong. Be okay with just being you and embrace life changes, and believe they are for the better.

If you feel alone because you are a consciously living person, remember the spirit that created you is always in you. Look at this amazing earth and the life it provides, which we sometimes take for granted. Usually when a person becomes spiritually awake, they let go of friends that are unconscious. This is okay. You don't owe anyone your life. This is *your* life. Spend more time alone to work on yourself.

Be sure to mix with society a little, even if you do not want to. It is better than becoming too isolated in oneself and getting depressed. Depression is most times part of awakening and losing fake happiness, to finding yourself by learning and unlearning all the conditioning of previous years. Anxiety is normal during this time. Take your time. Do not rush the process or you will be back at the start every time. Embrace this special journey back to you. When nervous, change your perception/feeling.

It is normal to be nervously excited about life in this time because you are a conscious person. Time will change this fear based nervousness. Being nervous is normal.

From time to time look down at your shoes and ask yourself if you are filling them with your unique self.

Rosses Point, Sligo

CHAPTER 25
Reflections

Religion

Any religion that sees us all as one is correct. It is our ego which says different. Any church or place that brings stillness and allows intuition to speak, that is the divine connection. You have to realize it for yourself. Any organization can teach you, but each soul is on a personal journey.

Being nice

Being nice is so rare. When you are genuinely nice, people think there is something wrong with you or that you have a hidden agenda. Sometimes we need a lot of healing before we learn what nice is because there are so many fake people in the world. It is normal for society to bring you down when you become spiritually awake. You will see everyone as an amazing gift of creation.

Every one of us is special. Even if you are on the street sleeping rough or live in a mansion, it is the same spirit of life in each of us. We are all just in a different place in life. It is up to yourself and your own responsibility to lead a pure life based on your creation and intuition.

Emotion

Any person that is big-hearted is very loving; sometimes giving too much love away. If the emotion of love is threatened in the person, the emotion can change to fear very fast. The thing is to be aware of this and balance emotions; breathe, observe and see the lesson. Do not try to be perfect as there is no such thing.

Attention Span

Our attention span is getting shorter and shorter due to phones, computers, and a fast paced life. Meditation, being out in nature, reading, exercise and hobbies are the cure!

Victim

Never see yourself as a victim. It is very easy to fall into this habit

80% of the time we are affected by noise around us in the world. The other 20% should be focused on stillness. Stillness is where the Source speaks. Increase time spent in the stillness of nature and pleasant prayer. You will learn, grow, heal and get answers with stillness. Embrace stillness and silence.

You have to have an attitude to enjoy life, even in situations you are not comfortable with. These are growth situations. Change your perception to growth and embrace change.

Authority

Sometimes authority in the home is incorrect. The child has authority over parents. Parents answer to the child instead of parents teaching the child basic manners, respect, boundaries, love, morals, right from wrong and greed from generosity. This sometimes comes from not teaching the child about life, but trying to buy a child their life; for example, no matter what education a child or adult had, if they do not know the basics in life, then no education is any good. The child will be brought up too self-centered. This causes all sorts of problems. It creates a void in a child, the parents and wider family which causes major problems. It takes unlimited amounts of work to undo this damage. Some people never recover. First thing that needs to be done is identify problems. Take responsibility; accept a lack of awareness from the child or adult, past situations and society. Look within for answers.

The Energy of Nature

It is important we stay in contact with the rhythm of nature because we are nature. When we are out in nature, in sunrise, away from the frantic traffic and the unconscious human activity; when we are really in the presence of nature in the early morning, you can sense nature slowly getting ready for the day. Being out early in nature balances us and sets our rhythm for the day, instead of waking up and walking straight into a frantic pace of life. In the modern world, as the day goes on it speeds up energy and the pace of life picks up. It slows down in the evening until darkness arrives for us to fully rest in harmony and get ready for another day. It is not possible to be working at night, rushing and racing. There is no point to it. It is insanity. People are being used and do not realize it.

It is only possible to experience life and enjoy it when in harmony with nature.

Value yourself. You have as much right as anyone else to be on this earth, and to experience your own freedom to be yourself. A lot of children are conditioned to think life is all about them, so when they get older everything is about them. We are all one. You can be the light, whether it is in a group, with family or when on our own. Be the light for humanity from a soul point of view and do not try to control other's lives. Be the one showing the light for humanity by example, with your boundaries and self-respect and love in place, you have it within you to shine.

Be conscious in life not to be attached to time. It is then we have freedom to live authentically.

Life can be like going to the cinema and getting captured by the movie. We can become captured by the politics of life. You are not the job, house or car. Nor are you somebody else's thoughts. You have to be your own person and the intelligence that created you. Anything that is love based is from our Source of Creation. Anything fear based is human mind conditioning and the opposite of our Creator.

Power of the Mind – Just from instructions in your mind, see what speed it can direct your body, arms, legs, head, feet, eyes and mouth! Now look at the speed of emotion and how it can direct the mind and body. To have balance in your life, you have to know yourself spiritually and the Intelligence that created you; you need to have awareness to your conditioning from this life and previous generations. In society everybody is exposed to brainwashing in so many ways. Know yourself through your feelings. Know your body and what it needs from nature and our elements - our source of everything. Learning to balance feelings in your body is important when you are a consciously living person. When your life is in balance with self and nature and correct people it is much easier for your Soul/Creator/Spirit of Intelligence to guide you. It is feeling that operates the mind 95% of the time, so when you feel The Amazing Creation that you are, then all the work of clearing and grounding is done. This is when the mind is in harmony. Everyone is special. Be yourself.

Imagine you witnessed an apparition; how amazing it would be? You are the living version of that apparition you experienced. You came from and are that spiritual source.

The gentleness of nature feeds our soul with a mildness to feel alive, and to feel free and at one with our Source and ourselves; and the endurance and strength of nature to produce such life. Nature is our soul.

You have to learn the spiritual love of our Source to feel love for yourself and everyone else on earth; to feel all that is true, love, peace and confidence. Celebrating the love of your own creation and all creation brings joy and harmony to life and peace into the world. Spiritual love is gratitude for the Source that created you and that gives you life. You do not take life; it is given to you with love. Be grateful for your creation.

Embrace your individuality and be conscious of how special you are. There is just one you.

When we observe the natural, pure strength and intelligence of nature on a daily basis, it aligns our subconscious mind to a natural state of being; because we are made from the elements of nature.

Trust your own power - When you learn to trust your own power within and when you get to know that power, you become an amazing force of nature. This power can never collapse because it is not ego and ego power is fleeting.

Learn the true voice, feeling and third eye within that is in harmony with your Source. Nourish your energy while you can with sleep and work. Resting is important, as is good food. Good company is very important. Do not replace this with cats or dogs - they are important, but people in life are more important.

Spend time in exercise, listening to music and nice sounds, and anything else that nourishes the soul.

The power of the elements; fire and sun gives all life. The power of fire in an engine to move a car, truck, or plane – this is an example of the power of fire within us all. We are an unlimited life force and we have to respect this.

We need space between people, and space for our body. In nature, if we are in an accident everything seems to go in slow motion; this comes from our Creator. Nature especially produces space in areas out of our control This is why it is important to try to live authentically, because if we are to try to control space in our lives, we are trying to control everything and life. It is a natural process. One thing to be conscious of is our breath when we are going through tough times. It regulates our nervous system.

Space is an important part of life. If you observe the space between waves it is as nice as the wave! There is a natural space in time, space in day and night, space in nature, space in breath. For anyone in an accident and going through trauma, time seems to slow as nature provides space to limit shock, to regulate the nervous system and to live authentically. Sometimes people feel empty. This is a different kind of space. It could be from too much being expected of people, constantly feeling that enough is never enough in this modern world. It could be from giving too much of themselves away for too long, to anything or anyone causing soul loss. It could be from going through traumatic times on heavy medication, drugs or alcohol. The soul doesn't want to experience pain, so it creates space for you to recognise that there is a problem by your feeling empty. You need to identify the problem and where it came from and begin healing to recover the soul.

I think the main habit in the world is a lack of human conscience. A lot of people do not know who they are, so the results are crisis after crisis from a habit built from not being aware of their conscience source of being

We don't have enough laughter in our lives, so sometimes we have to look for it. We should not forget to express ourselves in happy times, because sometimes things can be too serious for too long and we forget the importance of laughter and feeling good, to nourish ourselves and not take everything too serious and too personally.

Author Biography

Since I was a child playing in the fields, the trees and streams, setting potatoes and vegetables with my family, I have had a strong feeling of connection to all the elements; earth, water, air, fire and sun. It was only years later I understood that these elements have unlimited intelligence to produce all life and everything we need. These elements are part of our soul. From a young age I had a feeling of oneness and freedom in nature.

I worked hard all my life, but some years ago I ended up working for a company which was good, but followed the modern way too much. It was all about money and not enough about life.

I ended up going through a 'Dark night of the soul' for many years. I reconnected with nature - our soul, read a lot of books and gained a lot of spiritual healer friends whom I have listed in the Acknowledgements.

I feel this book is part of my purpose in life. This book is to guide people in all walks of life on the spiritual and human aspects of life and how special everyone is.

Kevin Ireland, March 2023.

Printed in Great Britain
by Amazon